Delivering Psycho-e
Evaluation Results to

Delivering Psycho-educational Evaluation Results to Parents presents a concrete and adaptable Feedback Model that efficiently communicates complex evaluation results to parents in an easily understandable manner.

The book discusses a model rooted in basic learning principles, effective communication practices, and practitioner empathy towards the parent experience of the home-school relationship, hinging upon practitioners and parents jointly creating a permanent product of the evaluation results during the feedback process. It provides early career school psychologists with a parent-friendly Feedback Model that can be adapted to their school-based setting. The text includes specific verbiage to explaining constructs in the cognitive, achievement, visual-motor, and social-emotional domains, along with considerations in application to working with diverse populations.

The text is intended for school psychologists and professionals who complete psycho-educational evaluations for special education eligibility. More specifically, the text is envisioned to support the graduate training of school psychologists and the professional development of early career professionals in the field.

Francis J. DeMatteo, EdD, NCSP, is a nationally certified school psychologist who has worked as a school psychologist practitioner and director of school psychology training programs. His research interests include family-school relations, providing feedback results to parents, and post-school transition.

Delivering Psycho-educational Evaluation Results to Parents

A Practitioner's Model

Francis J. DeMatteo

Routledge
Taylor & Francis Group

NEW YORK AND LONDON

First published 2021
by Routledge
52 Vanderbilt Avenue, New York, NY 10017

and by Routledge
2 Park Square, Milton Park, Abingdon, Oxon OX14 4RN

Routledge is an imprint of the Taylor & Francis Group, an informa business

© 2021 Taylor & Francis

Library of Congress Cataloging-in-Publication Data
A catalog record for this title has been requested

ISBN: 978-0-367-07484-5 (hbk)
ISBN: 978-0-367-07486-9 (pbk)
ISBN: 978-0-429-02097-1 (ebk)

Typeset in Bembo
by Newgen Publishing UK

To Lisa, my all.

Contents

Figures and Table

Figures

Table

Acknowledgments

Special thanks to the many school psychologists with whom I have worked throughout my career. You helped to keep me positive on the toughest of days.

Thank you to all the school psychologists that I have trained throughout the years. Your questions, feedback, and perspectives helped me to realize the value of my contribution to the profession.

Thank you to the Department of Psychology at Humboldt State University for your encouragement and support of this project.

Special thanks to Courtney Pack who contributed her time and efforts to portions of this book.

1 Introduction

Literature has consistently demonstrated that a positive home-school relationship is a critical component to students' overall success. When families and schools work together, students demonstrate more positive attitudes toward learning, higher achievement, and decreased behavioral problems while families obtain an understanding of educational practices and their function in supporting their children's learning (Christenson & Reschly, 2009; NASP, 2012). Educators must continuously nurture the home-school relationship so that it has the ability to endure times of high stress and potential conflict. As such, educators need to remain current in best practices, develop an operational sense of empathy toward student and family needs, and strive to communicate with families in a transparent and respectable manner.

The home-school relationship is most vulnerable at the time of feedback of multi-disciplinary evaluation results for potential eligibility for special education services. According to Federal Regulations, pre-kindergarten through grade 12 students who demonstrate academic and/or behavioral needs in the general education curriculum are entitled to a multi-disciplinary evaluation by qualified personnel (Federal Register, 2006). Following this evaluation, federal special education regulations and codes of professional ethics dictate that the multi-disciplinary team is then required to share the results and recommendations with the parents in a language that is easily understood (APA, 2017; Federal Register, 2006; NASP, 2010). However, asymmetry in parent-professional communication typically exists, as professionals talk differently to each other than to parents (Sands, 1988, 1994). Professionals speak in the "voice of science;" whereas, parents compose their thoughts from the "voice of the life world" (Sands, 1994).

The primary purpose of this text is to provide early career school psychologists and other practitioners who conduct psycho-educational evaluations with a concrete, parent-friendly Feedback Model that can be readily adapted to their school-based setting. This model is designed to facilitate parents' understanding of evaluation results; thereby increasing their functional knowledge of their child's strengths and needs and reducing the risk of future parent-school conflict. While doing so, the text aims to describe critical elements to the process of providing feedback of psycho-educational evaluation results to parents, as related to relevant literature and practices in the areas of assessment, home-school relationships, and parents of children with disabilities.

The text is organized in a hierarchical manner and it is recommended that the reader proceeds through the chapters in their designated order to obtain the necessary context of the Feedback Model and develop an awareness of the prerequisite skills to implement the model. References to parents in the text includes the child's primary caregiver and guardian; and it is assumed that school psychologists are charged with the responsibility to deliver feedback of psycho-educational evaluation results to parents, given school psychologists' extensive training in broad assessment principles and the administration, scoring, and interpretation of published norm-referenced standardized tests (PNRSTs). In the upcoming chapters, the underlying rationale of the Feedback Model and reasons that support its daily use are discussed (Chapter 2). Afterwards, the Information Processing Model of human learning is reviewed while relating its principles to the Feedback Model's infrastructure (Chapter 3). With this knowledge, parents' stressors and perceptions of the feedback meeting are discussed (Chapter 4) and prerequisite practitioner skills to utilizing the model are reviewed (Chapter 5). The Feedback Model is then presented in a detailed stepwise manner with specific verbiage for each step being provided (Chapter 6). Utilizing the model with diverse populations is subsequently reviewed (Chapter 7) and the text concludes with a discussion of applying the Feedback Model to two complex, real-life cases (Chapter 8).

Basic Premises to the Feedback Model

Basic premises to the Feedback Model are discussed in the following sections. These premises help to establish the perspective from which the model is intended to be utilized. The model can be readily implemented when providing feedback of psycho-educational results in a private clinical setting; however, this text will emphasize its use during school-based multi-disciplinary team meetings that occur following the multi-disciplinary evaluation of students for potential eligibility for special education services.

According to federal regulations, a student may qualify for special education services under one or more of thirteen disability categories following an evaluation by a multi-disciplinary team (Federal Register, 2006). The multi-disciplinary team consists of the student's parents, a regular education teacher, a special education teacher, a Local Educational Agency (LEA) representative, and a qualified evaluator specific to the disability area. When the primary reason for referral involves issues related to cognition, academic performance, and/or social-emotional and behavioral functioning, participation of a school psychologist and a subsequent psycho-educational evaluation are necessary.

Multi-disciplinary evaluations for potential special education eligibility typically involve a school psychologist and include a psycho-educational evaluation when the reason for referral is related to eligibility determination in the following federally defined disability categories: 1) Autism Spectrum Disorder, 2) Emotional Disturbance, 3) Intellectual Disability, 4) Multiple Disabilities, 5) Other-health Impairment, 6) Specific Learning Disability, and 7) Traumatic Brain Injury (Federal Register, 2006). With each of these disability categories, psycho-educational evaluations are necessary to determine eligibility because the essence of the disability is dependent on levels of cognitive, academic, social-emotional, and behavioral functioning.

Delivering psycho-educational evaluation results to parents during a multi-disciplinary team meeting is a delicate and complex process that involves multiple moving variables (DeMatteo, 2005). These variables are loosely categorized into five areas and consist of the parents' 1) history of interaction with the school, the 2) tone of past home-school communication, the 3) parents' perception of self and the 4) individual delivering the results, and 5) characteristics of the multi-disciplinary meeting, such as its length in time, physical environment, and number of individuals present. As a whole, these variables form the backdrop to which the Feedback Model is utilized and have the potential to influence parents' recep-tiveness to the content of the feedback results. The Feedback Model is intended to work within the conditions established by these variables and minimize their potential adverse effects on the parents' understanding and ultimate acceptance of the psycho-educational evaluation results.

A Guiding Premise to Delivering Feedback

Delivering feedback of psycho-educational evaluation results to parents is akin to a teacher instructing a classroom lesson with instructional goals and learning outcomes. Thus, to help frame the feedback process, consider the role of a class-room teacher. In a classroom setting, the teacher's role is to facilitate the student's acquisition of knowledge and skills in a particular topic area. To do so, the teacher must first consider the student's facility with related background information. If the student has prerequisite knowledge related to the topic, then he or she will have a "shared language" with the instructional process and a foundation to support the acquisition of new content. If the student does not have prerequisite knowledge of the topic, then the teacher must use explicit instructional methods and expose the student to the content information through utilizing lower-level learning objectives for cognitive tasks.

Learning objectives for cognitive tasks typically fall into one of following six hierarchical categories: Knowledge, Comprehension, Application, Analysis, Synthesis, and Evaluation (Bloom et al., 1956). At the Knowledge level, as a result of instruction, the student knows terms, facts, and procedures through defining, describing, and identifying information. At the Comprehension level, the stu-dent understands facts and principles by providing explanations, examples, and summaries. Skills are demonstrated at the Application level through the student's ability to use learned information in new and concrete situations and competency at the Analysis level requires the student to successfully break-down material into its component parts to understand their organizational structure. At the highest levels, the student is able to put together pieces of information to form a new whole (Synthesis) and judge the value of material for a given purpose (Evaluation). Because these categories are hierarchical, the student must demonstrate compe-tency with the content at the Knowledge level before he or she can be successful with learning at the higher levels and this principle holds true when progressing through the remaining categories.

As applied to the feedback process, school psychologists delivering the psycho-educational evaluation results must first determine the parent's "shared language," or level of prerequisite knowledge, related to the content to be discussed. By default, the school psychologist should assume that the parent has a minimal level of prerequisite knowledge related to the psycho-educational evaluation process for two reasons. First, terminology inherent to the products of a psycho-educational evaluation process is highly complex. Common terms such as cognitive skills, processing skills, cognitive efficiency, fluid reasoning, crystallized intelligence, executive functioning, and behavioral analysis are highly complex and it takes years of specialized formal training for one to develop the facility to operationally define these terms and apply them to a given set of circumstances. Second, parents might unintentionally overestimate their "shared language" with the psycho-educational evaluation process given their exposure to information obtained from what seems to be professional sources; information that is often not understood in the correct context. As society matures, communication mediums improve, and technological advances occur, individuals have access to information and knowledge in virtually any topic area. This access to information can be extremely beneficial and empowering, as it provides one with the ability to better identify resources and opportunities to improve one's circumstances. However, without the proper interpretation and prerequisite awareness, easy access to information and knowledge may provide some with self-perceptions that they are proficient in a particular area. Unbeknownst to these individuals, this proficiency is superficial in nature and, to a large degree, it can not substitute for professional training and experience in a particular field.

When school psychologists recognize the parent's lack of true prerequisite knowledge or "shared language" in the content area, then the hypothetical learning objectives for the feedback session should be written at the Knowledge level of learning. Instruction (i.e. feedback) at this level utilizes concrete prompts and vocabulary that is readily accessible to the learner (parent) and the goal of the feedback process is for the parent to leave the feedback session with the ability, in basic language, to correctly describe, identify, and label core terminology related to the psycho-educational evaluation process. Only after this ability is acquired will the parent be able to conceptualize his or her child in relation to this terminology and subsequent educational diagnosis if appropriate.

There will be circumstances in which feedback of psycho-educational evaluation results will need to be presented to parents who have a prerequisite knowledge of related concepts and terminology. These parents typically are in careers related to psychology, education, and mental health. In such cases, the school psychologist should continue with the objective of presenting the content of feedback at the Knowledge level. Doing so will preserve the parents' "cognitive capacity" and reinforce their understanding of concepts. It will also provide them with the opportunity to more actively engage in the feedback process through asking deeper-level questions specific to their child. Note that "cognitive capacity" refers to the inherent limitations of short-term working memory as described within the context of the Information Processing Model, or Dual-Store of human learning (Atkinson & Shiffrin, 1968, 1971; Baddeley, 1986). This model will be reviewed and applied to the hierarchy of cognitive tasks in Chapter 3: Human Learning.

Verbal Feedback: A Supplement

Federal regulations and ethical principles require that a formal report is generated and shared with parents following a multi-disciplinary evaluation for potential special education services (AERA, 2014; Federal Register, 2006; NASP, 2010). This evaluation report essentially contains information regarding the psycho-educational evaluation, the child's current levels of functioning as related to the educational setting, a rationale for determining the child's eligibility in satisfying one or more of 13 disability categories, and the child's degree-of-need to receive specialized instruction via an Individualized Education Plan.

Multiple sources offer recommendations for report writing (Michaels, 2006; Sattler, 2008; Walrath, Willis, Dumont, 2014). Of greatest importance among these recommendations, the report is to be written clearly and objectively for its intended target audience (i.e. parents, teachers, administrators). Abbreviations and jargon are to be avoided and sentences are to be short with each directly contributing to the overall purpose of the document. The report should be concise but adequate in length. Biased terms are to be eliminated and the child's levels of functioning are to be described from a strengths-based, rather than deficit approach. These recommendations are intended to improve the readability of the report and parents' understanding of its content. However, despite the best intentions of the report's author, the report serves as a legal document and is the final product of the evaluation process. Thus, it is typically lengthy and it has the risk of being written in a legalese tone with complex terminology, standard scores, and an abundance of details.

It is unfair to expect an individual, such as a parent who is not specifically trained in psycho-educational assessment, to understand the contents of a report without supplementary aids and assistance. These aids and assistance occur through the verbal feedback of the assessment results that accompany the report. Providing verbal feedback along with written report has been shown to help build therapeutic relationships and allow opportunity for questions to be answered more thoroughly (Allen, Montgomery, Tubman, Frazier, & Escovar, 2003). Thus, the Feedback Model presented in this text is intended to supplement, not supplant, the formal report that is generated at the conclusion of the evaluation process. In fact, as will be reviewed in Chapter 6: *Creating a Permanent Product with the Parent: Utilizing the Feedback Model*, an initial step in the feedback process is to describe the goal of the feedback meeting, which "is to provide parents with a snap-shot of the results, so that they can better understand the detailed report at their leisure during a later time."

Published Norm-Referenced Standardized Tests

Comprehensive psycho-educational evaluations are composed of four pillars of assessment-published norm-referenced standardized tests (PNRSTs), interviews, behavioral observations, and informal assessment procedures (Sattler, 2008). Each pillar provides a unique lens to view the child's level of functioning and data from each must be integrated to address the referral question. With less complicated cases, the data from each "hang-together" and are consistent in supporting a particular conclusion supported by the evaluation results. More commonly though, data from one or more pillars may not fully support the overall profile of results and the evaluator will need to critically consider the weight of the outlying data and whether or not it steers the evaluation to an alternate conclusion.

Data from appropriately administered and properly interpreted PNRSTs are robust and typically heavily weighted in a comprehensive psycho-educational evaluation for multiple reasons. Established PNRSTs are well researched and have adequate to above psychometric properties. PNRSTs efficiently quantify a child's level of functioning in multiple domains (i.e. cognition, reading, mathematics, written language, oral language, behavior) and they utilize standardized administration and scoring procedures to minimize examiner bias (Sattler, 2008). Furthermore, performance on PNRSTs is compared to a clearly defined norm group and subsequent results describe a child's performance as compared to his or her peer group (Sattler, 2008). Because of these reasons, results from PNRSTs are more complicated to explain, unlike those obtained from behavioral observation, interview, and informal assessment methods.

PNRST results create the cornerstones of the Feedback Model. Performance on each PNRST measure is systematically plotted on a defined grid in the presence of the parent. Afterwards, results from interviews, behavioral observations, and informal measures are plotted around the PNRST results yielding a comprehensive visual of the child's overall performance on the evaluation. This visual compels the evaluator to integrate the data obtained from the evaluation and allows the parent to actually *see* the underlying rational to a particular diagnosis, recommendation, or conclusion. *Seeing* this rationale, rather than simply *hearing* it, translates complicated abstract concepts into concrete information that is more easily understood by the parent. Thus, the evaluation process, results, and subsequent conclusions become more transparent to the parent. With improved transparency, the mystery that is often associated with a psycho-educational evaluation is likely reduced and the parent is in a better position to trust the evaluator and believe in the results obtained.

Standard Scores by Age

Results of PNRSTs represent an individual's performance when compared to peers in the norm group. These results can be presented through standard scores, percentile ranks, age-equivalents, and grade-equivalents and the comparison norm group can be defined by age or grade. Thus, the evaluation results might be expressed through standard scores and percentile ranks by age, standard scores and percentile ranks by grade, age-equivalents by age, and grade-equivalents by grade.

Using age and grade-equivalents in communicating an individuals' performance on a PNRST must be done with extreme caution, as these scores can be easily misinterpreted and misleading. Age-equivalent scores are obtained by calculating the average raw score on a particular measure by children at various ages; whereas, grade-equivalent scores are generated by computing the average raw score on a particular measure by children at various ages (Sattler, 2008). The fact that age and grade-equivalents represent an *average* raw score lead them to be only loose interpretations of performance when compared to the standardization sample. Sattler (2008) describes age and grade-equivalents as "psychometrically impure" and offers multiple explanations to this conclusion. These explanations include the following.

1) Age and grade-equivalent distributions are not necessarily representative of equal units. As such, the difference between a first grade-equivalent and second grade-equivalent may not be the same as the difference between a ninth grade and tenth grade-equivalent. Children grow and learn at different rates and skill acquisition typically occurs more rapidly at young ages.
2) Age and grade-equivalents are often products of interpolation and extrapolation; thus, the subsequent scores may not have been actually obtained by children in the norm sample.
3) Age and grade-equivalent scores are usually based on ordinal scales of measurement which do not have the capacity for calculation of the standard error of measurement.
4) Age and grade-equivalents are at risk for exaggerating small changes in performance. By increasing the raw score one or two points on a particular measure, the age and grade-equivalent might be increased by an entire chronological or academic year, respectively.

Similar to the impurities of age and grade-equivalents, standard scores and percentile ranks by grade are also imprecise. Any particular grade can have students who vary in one to three years of age depending on age of initial school entry and school retention practices. With these nuances of age and grade-equivalents and standard scores and percentile ranks by grade, it would seem most prudent for school psychologists to embrace the practice of using standard scores and percentile ranks by age when scoring, interpreting, and delivering feedback of psycho-educational evaluation results. The resulting product is more precise and explanation of "what the scores represent" is inherently less confusing.

The Feedback Model is designed to be used with standard scores and percentile ranks by age. More specifically, the model will rely on the categorical descriptions of standard scores by age (i.e. Average Range, Low Average Range, High Average Range, etc.) and the translation of these descriptive categories into easily-understood traits and behaviors. A detailed discussion of this process will be included in Chapter 5: *Prerequisite Practitioner Skills to Utilizing the Model.*

Summary

The current chapter provided an overview to the text and introduced basic premises that underlie the Feedback Model. The psycho-educational evaluation process was highlighted and feedback of evaluation results was described in terms of instructional objectives. Practitioners were reminded that verbal feedback of results is intended to supplement, not supplant, the formal psycho-educational report required by federal regulations and the utility of published norm-referenced standardized tests was emphasized. The chapter concluded with a discussion about the nuances of the representativeness of standardized scores and the Feedback Model was stated to utilize the categorical descriptions of standard scores by age.

References

Allen, A., Montgomery, M., Tubman, J., Frazier, L., & Escovar, L. (2003). The effects of assessment feedback on rapport-building and self enhancement process. *Journal of Mental Health Counseling, 25*, 165–182.

American Educational Research Association (2014). *Standards for educational and psychological testing.* American Educational Research Association.

American Psychological Association (2017). *Ethical principles of psychologists and code of conduct* (2002, Amended June 1, 2010 and January 1, 2017). Retrieved from www.apa.org/ethics/code/index.aspx

Atkinson, R. C. & Shiffrin, R. M. (1968). Human memory: A proposed system and its control processes. In K. W. Spence & J. T. Spence (Eds.), *The psychology of learning and motivation: Advances in research and theory* (Vol. 2). New York: Academic Press.

Atkinson, R. C. & Shiffrin, R. M. (1971). The control of short-term memory. *Scientific American, 225*, 2, 82–90.

Baddeley, A. D. (1986). *Working memory.* Oxford, England: Clarendon Press.

Bloom, B. S. (Ed.), Engelhart, M. D., Furst, E. J., Hill, W. H. & Krathwohl, D. R. (1956). *Taxonomy of educational objectives, handbook 1: The cognitive domain.* New York: David McKay Co.

Christenson, S. L., & Reschly, A. L. (Eds.). (2009). *Handbook of school-family partnerships.* New York, NY: Routledge, Taylor & Francis.

DeMatteo, F. J. (2005). *Predictors of parent satisfaction following multi-disciplinary evaluation for special education eligibility.* (Doctoral dissertation, Indiana University of Pennsylvania).

Federal Register (2006). *Part II. Department of Education: 34 CFR Parts 300 and 301. Assistance to states for the education of children with disabilities and preschool grants for children with disabilities; Final rule.* Retrieved from http://edocket.access.gpo.gov/2006/pdf/06-6656.pdf

Michaels, M. H. (2006). Ethical considerations in writing psychological assessment reports. *Journal of Clinical Psychology, 62*, 1, 47–58.

National Association of School Psychologists (2010). *Principles for professional ethics.* Retrieved from www.nasponline.org/standards/2010standards/1_%Ethical%20Principles.pdf

National Association of School Psychologists (2012). *School–family partnering to enhance learning: Essential elements and responsibilities* [Position Statement]. Bethesda, MD: Author.

Sands, R. G. (1988). Sociolinguistic analysis of a mental health interview. *Social Work, 33*, 149–154.

Sands, R. G. (1994). A comparison of inter-professional and team-parent talk of an interdisciplinary team. *Social Work in Education, 16*(4), 207–220.

Sattler, J. M. (2008). *Assessment of children: Cognitive foundations* (5th ed.). La Mesa, CA: Sattler.

Walrath, R., Willis, J. O., & Dumont, R. (2014). Best practices in writing assessment reports. In P. L. Harrison & A. Thomas (Eds.), *Best practices in school psychology: Data based and collaborative decision making.* Bethesda, MD: National Association of School Psychologists.

2   The Feedback Model's Necessity

The purpose of this chapter is to substantiate the need for a Feedback Model that can be utilized in the present by early career practitioners and grows with them in their practices as they professionally mature. As such, the role of the school psychologist will be discussed and ethical principles and federal regulations stating that practitioners are obliged to present findings in an understandable manner will be reviewed. Afterwards, relevant literature describing the feedback of assessment results with clinical and school psychologists will be discussed. As the topics of the chapter are presented, evidence will emerge to suggest the following theme. Although school psychologists spend the majority of their time in conducting psycho-educational evaluations, and legal and ethical guidelines indicate that the evaluation results and recommendations must be shared in a clear understandable manner with parents, school psychologists may receive only cursory training in this skill; and their ability to deliver feedback to parents is acquired tacitly through practicum, internship, and professional experiences.

The School Psychologist's Role

Definitions of school psychology as a profession have been noted since the 1920s and they began to develop in their specificity during the 1960s and 1970s (Fagan & Wise, 2007). As per NASP's webpage (www.nasponnline.org), the most current definition of a school psychologist is as follows.

> School psychologists help children and youth succeed academically, socially, and emotionally. They collaborate with educators, parents, and other professionals to create safe, healthy, and supportive learning environments for all students that strengthen connections between home and school. School psychologists are highly trained in psychology and education. They must complete a minimum of a post-master's degree program that includes a year-long internship and emphasizes preparation in mental health, child development, school organization, learning styles, and processes, behavior, motivation, and effective teaching. School psychologists must be certified and/or licensed by the state in which they work. They also may be nationally certified by the National School Psychology Certification Board (NSPCB).

In 2010, NASP released its formal Model of Practice to help guide school psychological service delivery and training (NASP, 2010a). This model identifies ten domains of practice that are organized into four broad categories of service delivery. These categories and domains are as follows.

Practices that Permeate all Aspects of Service Delivery

1) Data Based Decision Making and Accountability
2) Consultation and Collaboration

Direct and Indirect Services for Children, Families, and Schools

3) Interventions and Instructional Support to Develop Academic Skills
4) Interventions and Mental Health Services to Develop Social and Life Skills

Systems-Level Services

5) School-Wide Practices to Promote Learning
6) Preventative and Responsive Services
7) Family-School Collaboration Services

Foundations of School Psychological Service Delivery

8) Diversity in Development and Learning
9) Research and Program Evaluation
10) Legal, Ethical, and Professional Practice

NASP's ten domains of practice highlight the breadth of training for school psychologists and the potential roles and responsibilities that school psychologists can expect when working in the field. However, the amount of time that school psychologists practice within each domain is not necessarily equal. In other words, a school psychologist in District A may spend the majority of his or her time in completing psycho-educational evaluations for special-education eligibility (Data Based Decision Making and Accountability); whereas, the school psychologist in neighboring District B has his or her time primarily allocated to provide counseling services (Interventions and Mental Health Services to Develop Social and Life Skills) to at-risk students. As such, school psychologists' daily practice across the domains is largely determined by local policies, practices, and district administration's perception of school psychological service delivery (Fagan & Wise, 2007).

As a profession, school psychology has strong roots in the "test and place" model of service delivery wherein school psychologists spend the majority of their time conducting psycho-educational evaluations for special education eligibility determination. This is known as the "Traditional Model" of service delivery and it is the profession's default role and responsibility. Because of inefficiencies related to the traditional model that are beyond the scope of this text to discuss, the profession has been advocating for school psychologists to have a more diversified role and spend time practicing in domains other than assessment (Data

Based Decision Making and Accountability). Doing so, more adequately utilizes the school psychologist's skillset and better addresses the needs of children, families, staff, and administration.

Despite the profession's efforts to diversify the role of the school psychologist over the past 30 years, multiple reports suggest that school psychologists spend the greatest amount of their time in assessment related activities (Fagan & Wise, 2007). This conclusion is supported by numerous membership surveys that have been conducted by NASP. These membership surveys are typically robust and they are geographically representative of school psychology practice across the United States. Based on data from the 1994–1995 school year, "59.1% (n = 1922) of the respondents reported spending 70% of their time conducting special education evaluations" and "only 2.7% reported not completing special education evaluations" at all (Curtis, Hunley, Walker & Baker, 1999; p. 113). The authors further stated that these results were consistent with previous studies completed in the late 1970s through early 1990s.

Membership surveys during the past 20 years reflect a similar trend. In 1999, a randomly selected national sample (n = 370) of NASP members was asked to estimate the percentage of time that they were engaged in various professional activities (Bramlett, Murphy, Johnson, Wallingsford & Hall, 2002). Results indicated that respondents spent almost half of their time conducting assessments (46%) and the remaining time in activities such as consultation (16%), intervention (13%), counseling (8%), and conferencing (7%). Time spent in the professional activities of supervision, in-servicing, research, and parent training was less than 5 percent. Similarly in 2010, respondents to NASP's national membership survey (n = 1272) indicated that they spent 47.01 percent of their time conducting initial and re-evaluations for special education eligibility (Castillo, Curtis, Chappel & Cunningham, 2011); and in 2015, respondents (n = 1274) rated themselves to engage in individual evaluations to determine special education eligibility "*Quite a bit*" (m = 3.31) on a zero to four scale (0 = Not at all; 1 = Rarely; 2 = Somewhat; 3 = Quite a bit; 4 = Great Deal; Walcott, Charvet, McNamara & Hyson, 2016).

Given the history of the profession and the results of multiple national membership surveys, it seems safe to assume that conducting psycho-educational evaluations is a primary responsibility of school psychologists. Conducting evaluations though does not occur in isolation, as school psychologists are obligated to effectively communicate the evaluation's results.

Professional Ethics and Federal Regulations

School psychology is a unique profession in that we are subject to oversight by multiple professional organizations (i.e. NASP, APA, AERA), federal educational regulations, and individual states' interpretations of those regulations. To add further complexity, our primary certificate to practice in the public schools is granted through the state department of education, rather than through a professional regulatory board specific to the profession. With these circumstances, school psychologist practitioners need to remain current in the professional ethics and regulations of multiple bodies. Fortunately, these ethics and regulations are consistent in their message in regard to providing feedback of psycho-educational evaluation results to parents. Simply stated, parents need to be provided with the psycho-educational evaluation results and subsequent recommendations in a clear and understandable manner. A review of these ethical principles and regulations follows.

NASP's Ethical Principles

NASP's Principles for Professional Ethics is organized according to four broad themes (NASP, 2010b). These themes are: 1) Respecting the Dignity and Rights of All Persons, 2) Professional Competence and Responsibility, 3) Honesty and Integrity in Professional Relationships, and 4) Responsibility to Schools, Families, Communities, the Profession, and Society. Each of these themes is comprised of ethical principles which are then composed of specific standards. Although ethical principles in each of these themes can be indirectly related to feedback of results following psycho-educational evaluation, Principle II.3 Responsible Assessment and Intervention Practices within the Professional Competency Theme is most applicable. Under Principle II.3, Standard II.3.8 specifically states, "School psychologists adequately interpret findings and present results in clear, understandable terms so that the recipient can make informed choices" (NASP, 2010b, p. 8).

APA's Ethical Principles of Psychologists and Code of Conduct

APA's Ethical Principles of Psychologists and Code of Conduct is built upon five General Principles. These Principles are 1) Beneficence & Nonmaleficence, 2) Fidelity & Responsibility, 3) Integrity, 4) Justice, and 5) Respect for People's Rights and Dignity (APA, 2017). Ten ethical standards then emerge from the five Broad Principles as a whole. Standard 9.10 Assessment-Explaining Evaluation Results is directly related to providing feedback results following a psych-educational evaluation. This standard specifically states the following.

> Regardless of whether the scoring and interpretation are done by psycho-logists, by employees or assistants, or by automated or other outside services, psychologists take reasonable steps to ensure that explanations of results are given to the individual or designated representative unless the nature of the relationship precludes provision of an explanation of results (such as in some organizational consulting, pre-employment or security screenings, and forensic evaluations), and this fact has been clearly explained to the person being assessed in advance.
>
> (APA, 2017, p. 14)

AERA Standards for Educational and Psychological Testing

The American Educational Research Association's (AERA) Standards for Educational and Psychological Testing is a product of the collaboration between AERA, the American Psychological Association (APA) and the National Council on Measurement in Education (NCME; AERA, 2014). The *Standards for Educational and Psychological Testing* is intended to "promote sound testing practices and to provide a basis for evaluating the quality of those practices" (AERA, 2014, p. 1). As such, the text is aimed to support test developers, test consumers, and those who "interpret, or evaluate the technical quality of test results" (p. 1). The *Standards for Educational and Psychological Testing* differs from NASP and APA's Ethical Principles in that it specifically addresses one domain of school psychologists' daily functioning (Assessment/Data Based Decision Making and Accountability), rather than school psychologists' practice as a whole.

Within the *Standards for Educational and Psychological Testing*, Standard 6.10, in the cluster of *Reporting and Interpretation* of test results, is specifically relevant to school psychologists providing feedback of psycho-educational evaluation results to parents. Standard 6.10 states:

> When test score information is released, those responsible for testing programs should provide interpretations appropriate to the audience. The interpretations should describe in simple language what the test covers, what scores represent, the precision/reliability of the scores, and how scores are intended to be used.
> (AERA, 2014, p. 119)

Individuals with Disabilities Education Act: Section 300

Because school psychologists spend large portions of their time conducting evaluations related to special education eligibility and students' progress in specialized programs, much of their daily practice is governed by Section 300 of the Individuals with Disabilities Education Act (IDEA; Federal Register, 2006). IDEA is a federal law that defines the 13 disability categories, procedures for development of Individual Education Plans (IEP), district responsibilities, and parents' and students' due process rights. Based on this law, each state develops their special education regulations which then in turn are formally adopted by Local Education Agencies (LEAs). As such, individual states and LEAs may include additional requirements in their regulations that expand upon the federal IDEA statute.

Unlike the APA and NASP ethics and AERA's *Standards for Educational and Psychological Testing*, IDEA regulations do not have an individual standard explicitly stating that parents are to be provided with feedback of psycho-educational evaluation results in a clear and understandable manner. However, multiple sections of the document dictate that parents must be inherently involved in the evaluation process from the time of providing consent for the evaluation through the time of developing the child's educational program after considering the evaluation results. Furthermore, the regulations stipulate that all communication with parents during the child's evaluation process must occur in their native language and in a manner that the parent understands. A review of IDEA regulations specific to parents and the multi-disciplinary evaluation process follows.

Section 300.9 Consent

"The parent has been fully informed of all information relevant to the activity for which consent is sought, in his or her native language."
(Federal Register, 2006, p. 46757)

Section 300.29 Native Language

Native language, when used with respect to an individual who is limited English proficient, means the following: 1) the language normally used by the individual, or, in the case of the child, the language normally used by the parents of the child.

(Federal Register, 2006, p. 46759–46760)

Section 300.322 Parent Participation

Each public agency must take steps to ensure that one or both of the parents of a child with a disability are present at each IEP team meeting or are afforded the opportunity to participate. The public agency must take whatever action is necessary to ensure that the parent understands the proceedings of the IEP team meeting, including arranging for an interpreter for parents with deafness or whose native language is other than English.

(Federal Register, 2006, p. 46788–46789)

Section 300.501 Opportunity to Examine Records, Parent Participation in Meetings

The parents of a child with a disability must be afforded the opportunity to participate in meetings with respect to i) The identification, evaluation, and educational placement of the child, and ii) The provision of FAPE [Free and Appropriate Public Education] to the child.

(Federal Register, 2006, p. 46791)

Providing Psycho-Educational Evaluation Results to Parents: Literature Review

As a science, the discipline of school psychology is built upon decades of quantitative and qualitative research that continues to be refined through the peer-review process and improvements in measurement techniques and our understanding of how parents and children interface with home, school, and community. This research informs policy-makers, advises training programs, and guides daily professional practice. It also provides the infrastructure to discipline specific reference texts and training manuals. As such, the literature in our field represents the "pulse of our practice" and the amount of scholarly publications dedicated to a particular professional topic in our field becomes an indicator of the topic's significance. With this rationale, it is not surprising that school psychology literature is dominated by research exploring the ecology of the profession, school-psychologists' daily roles and responsibilities, demographics of the profession, evidence based interventions, assessment, consultation, and behavior management.

In their 2016 article, Liu and Oakland explored the scholarly literature that specifically referenced the terms "school psychology" in the Science Citation Index from 1907 through 2014. Using scientometric analyses and HistCite and Pajek software, 4806 scholars were identified who contributed to 3260 articles in 311 journals from around the world. The majority of articles were published by authors in the United States and in 20 journals including the *Journal of School Psychology*, *Psychology in the Schools*, *School Psychology Review*, *School Psychology International*, and *School Psychology Quarterly*. Of this analysis, the following theme emerged from articles published between 2005 and 2009—56 percent of the articles discussed professional issues, 21 percent reviewed intervention practices, 20 percent addressed assessment, and 3 percent were related to consultation issues (Liu & Oakland, 2016). These results demonstrate the significant role that assessment plays in school psychology practice, as the topic has consumed a considerable amount of researchers' scholarly productivity.

Despite the popularity of assessment as a theme in school psychology literature, only a minimum number of studies specifically address providing feedback of assessment results to parents or clients following an evaluation. With many studies, feedback of evaluation results is discussed as an issue related to parent perceptions of the special education process (Fish, 2008; Spann, Kohler & Soenksen, 2003), parent participation in IEP development (Hyatt, 2004; Mcgarry Klose, 2010), family-school partnerships (Graybill, Esch, Vinoski, Truscott, Torres, Daniel, Crenshaw & Crimmins, 2016; Minke, 2010; Shridevi Subba Rao, 2000), and parent perceptions of their children with a disability (Lovitt & Cushing, 1999; Ryndak, Downing, Morrison, & Williams, 1996). Alternatively, other studies and publications discuss the feedback process as related to clinical psychologists' practice. Consider the following examples.

Delivering feedback of assessment results has been explored among practitioners in the clinical setting. In Finn and Tonsager's 1992 study, the benefits of sharing Minnesota Multiphasic Personality Inventory-2 (MMPI-2) results with a randomly selected sample of clients from a college counseling center was investigated. Thirty-two clients received feedback according to a collaborative model and 29 clients received only examiner attention. The clients who received feedback according to the collaborative model reported a significant decline in symptomatic distress and an increase in self-esteem, and felt more hopeful about their problems, both immediately following the feedback and at a two-week follow-up session. Also, the client's subjective impressions of the feedback session were overwhelmingly positive. Although the study failed to identify specific client variables or elements of the feedback session that were related to these changes, the findings suggested that psychological assessment can be used as a therapeutic intervention.

Similarly, a later study conducted a national survey of psychologists' training and practice in sharing distressing results with clients (Mercer, Hanson, & Poston, 2010). The study noted that to date, no studies have examined how, or whether, psychologists are trained to share distressing news with clients. A total of 329 licensed psychologists and American Psychological Association members were surveyed. Results suggested that 1) psychologists were significantly more reluctant to share "bad news" versus "good news," 2) anxiety accounted for approximately 30 percent of the variance in their reluctance to share "bad news," and 3) three-out-of-four psychologists share distressing news "to some extent" or more typically related to a client's psychological health, major psychological diagnosis, or learning disability. Findings also suggested that most psychologists are not trained to share distressing news, with only approximately 3 percent of the sample being familiar with existing recommendations and guidelines; and anxiety, concerns for self/other, context, and norms playing important roles in determining whether or not distressing news is shared with the client.

Other literature specifically related to clinical psychologists' feedback practices conceptualizes ten fundamental elements to the feedback process (Pope, 1992). Within the article, the author recognizes that "feedback may be the most neglected aspect of assessment" and that clear communication is paramount throughout the entire process (p. 268). The article states that "feedback is a dynamic, inter-active process that is an aspect of the larger process of assessment, and that the assessment often continues during the feedback session" (p. 268). At the time of initial meeting, roles and tasks of those participating in the process must be clearly communicated so that the client is aware of his/her rights related to informed consent and refusal and the protocol that may occur if a crisis situation is identi-fied. Familiarity with roles and tasks of the process also helps the client avoid con-fusion after learning of the results, as the client is better prepared to interact with the potential diagnoses and their respectable outcomes. The article recommended that clinicians must intentionally plan to frame the feedback in a manner that allows for the implications of the results to be interpreted without bias. As such, the clinician must recognize the fallibility of the results and be vigilant towards potential countertransference on behalf of the client. A detailed written report of the assessment process and results was also noted to serve as a valuable supplement to verbal feedback for clients, as it reminds them of important points that they may need to follow-up with during future sessions.

Additional research has explored psychologists' feedback training, supervision, and practice with North American samples (Curry & Hanson, 2010; Jacobson, Hanson, & Zhou, 2015). In the earlier study utilizing a national sample of clin-ical, counseling, and school psychologists from the United States, 35 percent of the respondents indicated that they provide verbal feedback of results every time following assessment and approximately 92 percent of the sample reported to give verbal feedback some of the time (Curry & Hanson, 2010). Slightly less than 3 percent of the sample stated to never provide feedback and there was a negative correlation between years since graduation and providing feedback for clinical psychologists. Most surprisingly, one-third of the sample reported that coursework, practicum, and internship were of "little to no help" in preparing them to provide feedback and these respondents cited self-instruction and "trial and error" as the primary means in which they learned feedback skills. A later study employing a Canadian sample yielded somewhat similar results (Jacobson, Hanson, & Zhou, 2015). With the Canadian respondents, 91 percent of psychologists indicated to frequently provide feedback following assessment, 25 percent reported that training in psychological assessment inadequately prepared them to provide feed-back, and 13 percent stated that training specific to the feedback process was inad-equate (Jacobson, Hanson, & Zhou, 2015).

Literature from clinical psychology describes feedback as a component to the therapeutic process and it supports the notion of feedback as an essential element to the assessment process rather than an entity in-and-of-itself. Clinicians routinely provide verbal feedback of results; yet their training specific to the practice is often perceived to be unhelpful or ineffective. Thus, many practitioners learn how to deliver verbal feedback through trial and error and self-instruction. Furthermore, clinicians may avoid feedback because of a reluctance to "share bad news" with the client and a specific Feedback Model was not identified; although essential components to the feedback process were offered. These broad themes seem relatively consistent with those that emerge from the school psychology literature.

A review of the past 30 years of school psychology literature yielded three publications in which researchers explicitly describe the feedback process with parents of children and adolescents. Although the first two publications occurred 20 years apart, both recognized the need for continued research in the area, promoted a collaborative approach to providing assessment feedback to parents, and acknowledged clinicians' general apprehension towards providing feedback (Pollak, 1988; Tharinger, Finn, Hersh, Wilkinson, Christopher, & Tran, 2008). Most importantly though, the articles reflected on the dynamics of the parent-clinician interaction during feedback and offered specific recommendations for clinicians to utilize when providing feedback to parents. As such, both articles help establish the foundation to the Feedback Model that will be later described in Chapter 6: *Creating a Permanent Product with the Parent: Utilizing the Feedback Model*.

Pollak's (1988) publication, which was later described "to be ahead of its time," noted how feedback with parents is considered a "problematic aspect of clinical work" with children and required "considerable thought, sensitivity, and skill on the part of the clinician" (p. 152). Pollack described the goals of the feedback process to be as follows: 1) improve overall understanding of the child's current levels of functioning and needs, 2) introduce and address adaptive coping as a product of learning unanticipated information regarding the child's functioning, and 3) establish the foundation for appropriate intervention. Feedback conferences were recommended to be preceded by one or two initial meetings with parents prior to the assessment with the child in order to obtain the necessary background information and establish trust and rapport with the parent. This trust and rapport later then help to circumvent parental resistance which may occur after their learning of potentially anxiety-provoking information within the assessment results. Although the specific format of the feedback process was recommended to be flexible based on the dynamics of the case, several guidelines were offered to nourish the collaborative partnership between the clinician and parent to facilitate a positive outcome. These guidelines were as follows:

1) Whenever possible, feedback should include family members influential in the child's life.
2) Feedback meetings should be organized around a specific time limit and stated to parent beforehand to help reduce parental anxiety.
3) As the meeting proceeds, active participation on behalf of the parents is to be encouraged to help parents achieve a coequal status.
4) A brief review of the information and concerns that were discussed during the initial interviews and prompted the evaluation.
5) A brief description of work with the child and a rationale for the diagnostic tests used.

6) As related to the assessment data, a review of recommendations with parent input.
7) Discussion regarding how the results and recommendations will be shared with the child if he/she was not present during the feedback meeting.

In addition to these seven basic guidelines, Pollak (1988) recognized the affective nature of feedback and its ability to provoke dormant intra and inter-psychic conflicts with parents related to self-esteem, dependency, and autonomy. As such, feedback should be crafted to the parents' demographic characteristics (e.g. intellectual abilities, educational background, fluency with psychological assessment) and clinicians are to avoid overloading parents with information to avoid confusion and inadvertently reinforce potential parental resistance to the findings. Disclosure of sensitive results or information that parents might perceive to be threatening should occur later in the meeting after the sharing of innocuous findings and the clinician should attempt to reframe or redefine any problems to promote emphatic understanding of the child.

Tharinger et al. (2008) built upon Pollak's (1988) work while having the goal of developing a "fully articulated collaborative model for providing assessment feedback to parents and children" (p. 601). Their publication reviewed suggestions from the literature for providing feedback to parents and children, collaborative approaches to assessment feedback, a rationale for providing feedback, assumptions and principles underlying the collaborative model of feedback, and how clinicians should prepare for assessment feedback with parents. Afterwards, they offered the following steps to provide structure to the parent feedback meeting.

1) Check-in with family members while being mindful of the anxiety-provoking nature of the meeting.
2) Review an agenda for the meeting and explicitly encourage parent input.
3) Share appreciations of the family thanking them for their participation and verbally noting any feelings of frustration or confusion on behalf of all parties involved.
4) Review assessment results.
5) Review recommendations.
6) Closing the session, elicit reactions, check for comprehension, discuss future contacts, and sharing what the clinician learned.

Of particular note with Tharinger et al.'s (2008) publication is their reference to self-verification theory (Swan, 1996, 1997) and emphasis on family stories and narratives. Essentially, a family story is how one perceives the family as a unit along with his or her roles and responsibilities within the system. All families have a "story" and each member's role within the story is developed from a history of experiences and interactions that occur against the backdrop of others' perceptions, beliefs, and values within the family. These stories, which help to organize our perceptions, interpret past experiences, and emotionally connect us to family members (Swan, 1996), serve as schemas that we use to navigate the world. Our schemas are highly resistant to change and we tend to be drawn to information and individuals that confirm our "story" and resist that which does not; hence, a description of the self-verification theory. As applied to the feedback process, parents are provided with influential information that they have not yet included in their family story. They are most likely to include this information in their story, rather than resist, if they have a collaborative relationship with the clinician who is sharing the results. Thus, through emphasizing parent participation in feedback meetings and perceiving them to be co-equal partners in the assessment and generation of recommendations, parents are less likely to be resistant to assessment outcomes and better able to make sense of the assessment results.

Tharinger et al.'s (2008) publication also provides guidelines that specifically address the order in which assessment results should be presented to parents during the feedback meeting to help avoid the self-validation effect. Borrowing from Schroeder, Hahn, Finn, and Swann's (1993) work, Tharinger noted that clients are more likely to accept assessment feedback when it is ordered in a manner similar to parents' existing narratives. Thus, using recommendations from previous research (Finn, 1996), the presentation order of assessment results during feedback should occur according to Level 1, Level 2, and Level 3 classifications. Level 1 findings are presented first and they consist of assessment results that are closest to how parents already perceive their child. Presenting this information at the onset helps to lower parents' anxiety and reinforce that their perceptions of the child are supported by the assessment results. Level 2 findings consist of information that slightly challenges parents' perceptions of their child but does not threaten their self-esteem or values and beliefs. The bulk of the feedback session should address assessment results within this category, as clinicians attempt to reframe parents' perceptions of their child while referencing historical information and test data to help parents create a "new story." Level 3 findings should be presented later in the feedback session because findings within this category are discrepant from parents' perceptions of their child and may cause conflict, especially if the parents' perceptions of the child are essential in sustaining their own self-esteem. At this stage, clinicians continue to reframe parent beliefs about their child while working to debunk parents' myths about related topics. As these techniques are applied, parents are more likely to consider Level 3 information because the data presented earlier (Level 1 & Level 2) were consistent with parent perceptions of the child.

Glazer's (2014) more recent publication focused specifically on school psychologists' skill in communicating evaluation results to parents and emphasized consideration of *what* the school psychologist is communicating along with *how* he or she is sharing the results. Through emphasizing the *what* and *how* of the feedback process, Glazer (2014) essentially addresses the *content* and *process* of the feedback session. Content skills refer to the practitioner's factual knowledge base of assessment in general, the factor structure of the instruments, constructs measured by each instrument, and classification ranges for standardized scores. Alternatively, process skills consist of basic counseling techniques such as active listening, paraphrasing, summarizing, and reframing. Glazer addresses both content and process skills while referring to the written psycho-educational report that accompanies the assessment process. Note that the written psycho-educational report is not emphasized in the discussions of the Feedback Model that occur in Chapters 5 and 6. As you will see later, it is recommended that parents are provided the written psycho-educational report after the clinicians' verbal presentation of the assessment results to the parents. This practice is intentional, as providing the parents with the report prior to verbal presentation of results will likely attribute to the overloading of parents' short-term working memory. Remember that the written psycho-educational report serves as a legal document and despite practitioners' efforts to write it in a clear and understandable manner, it likely contains complex details, concepts, and language that parents perceive to be confusing. One of the purposes of the Feedback Model is to provide parents with a "snapshot" of the assessment results to better understand the written psycho-educational report when they are reading it at their leisure during a later time.

Glazer (2014) offered four key points to help practitioners prepare for the feedback session. These key points consisted of: 1) summarizing talking-points according to themes, strengths, and weaknesses, 2) making notes of important points to efficiently discuss assessment findings, 3) reviewing the standardized measures and scoring considerations to illuminate links between standardized tasks and daily functioning, and 4) allowing enough time for the feedback session to avoid parents feeling rushed and to allow for communication to be concise. Similar to other researchers (Tharinger, Finn, Hersh, Wilkinson, Christopher, & Tran, 2008), it was suggested that practitioners share positive attributes of the child at the start of the feedback session and then refer back to these attributes when discussing recommendations. Thus, assessment data should not be the sole focus of the meeting and practitioners should avoid presenting information in a subtest-by-subtest manner to avoid overwhelming and confusing the parents. Using a visual chart with qualitative descriptions was also advocated to aid in parents' understanding of standardized test data.

In addition to providing a priori tips, Glazer (2014) offered specific process related techniques for practitioners to help parents better understand the content of the feedback session. As such, practitioners were encouraged to reflect on their individual presentation skills, such as organization, clarity of ideas, voice inflection, and eye contact during the feedback session. Communication during the feedback session should be as clear and concise as possible and practitioners were recommended to attend to parents' nonverbal communication and actively check for understanding. Alert body posture and regular eye contact on behalf of the practitioner were mentioned and it was suggested that practitioners focus on themes of strengths and weakness rather than on scores and technical aspects of the assessment if the parent appears inattentive or overwhelmed by the depth of information. Most importantly, it was advised that practitioners avoid reading the psycho-educational report while presenting the results—a practice suspected to be regularly utilized by many to conform to the formalized nature of the feedback session, as it also serves as a special education eligibility determination meeting.

Summary

Chapter 2 reviewed literature regarding the roles and responsibilities of the school psychologist and highlighted professional ethical principles that compel practitioners to share assessment results with parents in a clear and understandable manner. Section 300 of IDEA was explored to identify how the federal special education regulations dictate that evaluation results should be shared with parents and relevant literature describing the feedback practices of clinical and school psychologists was discussed. The chapter concluded with a presentation of three publications that offered broad guidelines or steps for clinicians to implement when delivering feedback of assessment results to parents. These articles emphasized the benefits of a collaborative approach and contained strategies and techniques that are included in the Feedback Model that will be presented in Chapter 6: *Creating a Permanent Product with the Parent: Utilizing the Feedback Model.* In essence, practitioners conducting psycho-educational evaluations are ethically obligated to share the results with parents after evaluation of their child and feedback is a component inherent to the evaluation process, rather than an entity in-and-of-itself. National surveys suggest that most clinicians are not confident in their training to deliver feedback and many practitioners learn the skill through self-instruction and/or trial-and-error. Practitioners need to explicitly present opportunities during feedback for parents to perceive themselves as having "coequal status" and results should be presented in an order that gradually challenges "family stories." Despite collecting vast amounts of data during the evaluation process, practitioners must be prudent about the amount of information that is shared with parents during feedback in order to avoid them becoming overloaded which in turn leads to increased anxiety and potential conflict. Ultimately, the goal of the feedback session is for parents to leave the meeting with a solid understanding of the information presented and implications of the results so that they are enabled to actively participate in decision making processes regarding their children. Practitioners must utilize specific process related techniques to support the delivery of content information during the feedback session to realize this goal.

References

American Educational Research Association (2014). *Standards for educational and psychological testing.* Washington, DC: Author.

American Psychological Association (2017). *Ethical principles of psychologists and code of conduct* (2002, Amended June 1, 2010 and January 1, 2017). Retrieved from www.apa.org/ethics/code/index.aspx

Bramlett, R. K., Murphy, J. J., Johnson, J., Wallingsford, L., & Hall, J. D. (2002). Contemporary practices in school psychology: A national survey of roles and referral problems. *Psychology in the Schools, 39,* 327–335.

Castillo, J. M., Curtis, M. J., Chappel, A., & Cunningham, J. (2011). *School psychology 2010: Results of the national membership survey.* Bethesda, MD: National Association of School Psychologists. Retrieved from www.nasponline.org/.../Mbr_Survey_Results_2011_Conv_Session.pdf

Curry, K. T. & Hanson, W. E. (2010). National survey of psychologists' test feedback training, supervision, and practice: A mixed methods study. *Journal of Personality Assessment, 92,* 327–336.

Curtis, M. J., Hunley, S. A., Walker, K. J., & Baker, A. C. (1999). Demographic characteristics and professional practices in school psychology. *School Psychology Review, 28,* 104–116.

Fagan, T. K. & Wise, P. S. (2007). *School psychology past, present, and future* (3rd· ed.). Bethesda, MD: National Association of School Psychologists.

Federal Register (2006). *Part II. Department of Education: 34 CFR Parts 300 and 301. Assistance to states for the education of children with disabilities and preschool grants for children with disabilities; Final rule.* Retrieved from http://edocket.access.gpo.gov/2006/pdf/06-6656.pdf

Finn, S. E. (1996). *Using the MMPI-2 as a therapeutic intervention.* Minneapolis, MN: University of Minneapolis Press.

Finn, S. E., & Tonsager, M. E. (1992). Therapeutic effects of providing MMPI-2 test feedback to college students awaiting therapy. *Psychological Assessment, 4*(3), 278–287.

Fish, W. W. (2008). The IEP meeting: Perceptions of parents of students who receive special education services. *Preventing School Failure, 53*, 8–14.

Glazer, A. (2014). Communication matters: Effective oral communication of evaluation results. *Communique, 42*(6). Retrieved from www.nasponline.org

Graybill, E., Esch, R. C., Vinoski, E., Truscott, S., Torres, A., Daniel, K., Crenshaw, M., & Crimmins, S. (2016). Including the family member in interdisciplinary team meetings: Communication trend analysis. *Small Group Research, 47*(1), 3–27.

Hyatt, K. (2004). IEP Team meetings: A guide to participation for parents. *Helping Children at Home and School II: Handouts for Families and Educator.* Bethesda, MD: National Association of School Psychologists.

Jacobson, R. M., Hanson, W. E., & Zhou, H. (2015). Canadian psychologists' test feedback training and practice: A national survey. *Canadian Psychology, 56*, 394–404.

Liu, S. & Oakland, T. (2016). The emergence and evolution of school psychology literature: A scientometric analysis from 1907 through 2014. *School Psychology Quarterly, 31*, 104–121.

Lovitt, T. C., & Cushing, S. (1999). Parents of youth with disabilities: Their perceptions of school programs. *Remedial and Special Education, 20*(3), 134–142.

McGarry Klose, L. (2010). Special education: A basic guide for parents. *Helping Children at Home and School III.* Bethesda, MD: National Association of School Psychologists.

Merker, B. M., Hanson, W. E., & Poston, J. M. (2010). National survey of psychologists' training and practice in breaking bad news: A mixed methods study of the MUM effect. *Journal of Clinical Psychology in Medical Settings, 17*, 211–219.

Minke, K. (2010). Family-school conferences: A guide for parents and teachers. *Helping children at home and school III: Handouts for families and educators.* Bethesda, MD: National Association of School Psychologists.

National Association of School Psychologists. (2010a). *Model for comprehensive and integrated school psychological services.* Bethesda, MD: Author. Retrieved from www.nasponline.org/standards/2010standards/2_PracticeModel.pdf

National Association of School Psychologists. (2010b). *Principles for professional ethics.* Bethesda, MD: Author. Retrieved from www.nasponline.org/standards/2010standards/1_%20Ethical%20Principles.pdf

Pollak, J. M. (1988). The feedback process with parents in child and adolescent psychological assessment. *Psychology in the Schools, 25*, 143–153.

Pope, K. S. (1992). Responsibilities in providing psychological test feedback to clients. *Psychological Assessment, 4*, 268–271.

Ryndak, D. L., Downing, J. E., Morrison, A. P., & Williams, L. J. (1996). Parents' perceptions of educational settings and services for children with moderate or severe disabilities. *Remedial and Special Education, 17*(2), 106–118.

Rao, S. S. (2000). Perspectives of an African-American mother on parent–professional relationships in special education. *Mental Retardation, 38*, 475–488.

Schroeder, D. G., Hahn, E. D., Finn, S. E., & Swann, W. B., Jr. (1993). *Personality feedback has more impact when mildly discrepant from self-views.* Paper presented at the fifth annual convention of the American Psychological Society, Chicago, IL.

Spann, S. J., Kohler, F. W., & Soenksen, D. (2003). Examining parents' involvement in and perceptions of special education services: An interview with families in a parent support group. *Focus on Autism and Other Developmental Disabilities, 18*(4), 228–237.

Swan, W. B. (1996). *Self-traps.* New York: Freeman.

Swan, W. B. (1997). The trouble with change: Self-verification and allegiance to the self. *Psychological Science, 8,* 177–180.

Tharinger, D. J., Finn, S. E., Hersh, B., Wilkinson, A., Christopher, G. B., & Tran, A. (2008). Assessment feedback with parents and preadolescent children: A collaborative approach. *Professional Psychology: Research and Practice, 39*(6), 600–609.

Walcott, C. M., Charvet, J., McNamara, K. M., & Hyson, D. M. (2016). *School psychology at a glance: 2015 member survey results.* Bethesda, MD: National Association of School Psychologists. Retrieved from www.nasponline.org/.../Membership%20Survey%202015%20Handout.pdf

3   Human Learning

Successfully delivering feedback of assessment results to parents occurs within the natural limitations of human learning. Although human learning has been operationalized through numerous theories and complex definitions virtually since the beginning of time, it is best conceptualized through the Information Processing Model (IPM) when addressing the acquisition of content through cognitive tasks. As such, Chapter 3 will provide an overview of the Information Processing Model (IPM) and discuss the sensory register, short-term working memory, and long-term memory in terms of capacity, length of time information is stored in each component, and modality in which the information is stored. Afterwards, the role of short-term working memory and its limitations will be highlighted and applied to the Feedback Model's structure. Through familiarity with the IPM and role and limitations of short-term working memory, clinicians are better able to navigate the feedback session with parents—presenting parents with the most important of the assessment results without unintentionally overloading their ability to process the intended message.

Research from developmental, cognitive, and social psychology is consistent in its message that human beings are essentially "cognitive misers," as our default mode of functioning is to typically use the least amount of cognitive resources to navigate our daily world. We consistently rely on schemas to quickly make decisions and guide our social interactions. We tend to avoid materials that are unorganized or lack meaning; and we spend much of our time in concrete-operational thought, saving our formal-operational thinking skills for problem-solving specific to our area of expertise such as our profession. One might speculate that humans are cognitive misers because of hard-wired limitations inherent to our consciousness. These limitations are best explained in context through a review of the Information Processing Model of Learning.

The Information Processing Model

With the interest in cognitivism during the 1960s, researchers expanded on theories of memory introduced during the 1890s and proposed the dual-store model of memory (Atkinson & Shiffrin, 1968, 1971; Ormrod, 2008). The dual-store model is also known as the information processing model to some because of its similarity to an information selection and storage system—the modern-day personal computer. The information processing model is the most prevalent view of human memory and it is characterized by three distinct components: sensory register, short-term working memory, and long-term memory (Atkinson & Shiffrin, 1968, 1971; Ormrod, 2008).

In essence, with the information processing model, environmental stimuli first enter the sensory register where it is stored for a few seconds at most. If the stimuli are consciously attended to, then they move to short-term working memory and are stored for less than a minute. Within short-term working memory, the stimuli need to be processed further to move to long-term memory where they are permanently stored. The short-term working memory is the key component to this model. If the stimuli from the sensory register enters short-term working memory and are not processed any further, then the stimuli are forgotten. Alternatively, if the stimuli from the sensory register are processed further in short-term working memory, then it often requires retrieval of information stored in long-term memory. Thus, the short-term working memory needs to be "big enough" to process stimuli continuously arriving from the sensory register, retrieve relevant information from long-term memory, relate the new stimuli to retrieved information, and then label the new concept and store it in long-term memory. The capacity, duration, and modality of storage for each component of the information processing model will be described in the following sections. Especially note the characteristics of short-term working memory, as short-term working memory is fundamentally our consciousness that is the bottle-neck between the sensory register and long-term memory.

Sensory Register

Environmental stimuli are collected from our sensory organs (visual, auditory, tactile, kinesthetic, olfactory) and first stored in our sensory register. The capacity of the sensory register is likely to be unlimited and all of the information that we are capable of sensing is stored here in the same form that it was acquired: visual input stored in a visual form, auditory input stored in an auditory form; etc. (Ormrod, 2008). The duration of time that information is stored in the sensory register has been difficult to identify because the information moves to short-term working memory once it is processed and is asked to be reported upon (Ormrod, 2008). Regardless, early studies suggest that visual information appears to remain in the sensory register for less than one second and auditory information seems to last longer with a duration of two to four seconds (Darwin, Turvey, & Crowder, 1972; Loftus & Loftus, 1976). The rapid disappearance of information from the sensory register is likely due to interference, where new information replaces original information, and decay, where the information simply fades away over time (Loftus & Loftus, 1976; Willingham 2004).

The characteristics of sensory register are routinely evident in a classroom setting. Consider when an instructor calls upon a student who was clearly not paying attention, but the student was able to recite the last few words of the lecture back to the instructor. The student's ability to successfully accomplish this task was due to the information remaining in his or her sensory register for two to four seconds. If the instructor truly wanted to "catch" the student being inattentive, he or she would wait four seconds after speaking and then ask for the student to repeat the content.

Short-Term Working Memory

Short-term working memory consists of our consciousness where information is attended to, stored for a brief time, and processed (Atkinson & Shiffrin, 1968; Baddeley, 1986; Han & Kim, 2004). As such, short-term working memory is where "thinking" occurs and our central executer resides (Baddeley, 1986, 2001; Demetriou, Christou, Spanoudis, & Platsidou, 2002; Ormrod, 2008). The central executer has been popularly referred to as the "conductor of our brain" and it controls and monitors the flow of information throughout the memory system through the use of selective attention. Because of the central executer, we are able to selectively attend to information from our sensory register, determine what needs to be done with that information, retrieve relevant information from our long-term memory, relate the information from our sensory register to that of our long-term memory, and then store the new concept in our long-term memory. Overall, the central executer is the entity that is responsible for our ability to self-regulate our thoughts, emotions, and actions and it can be adversely influenced by substance use and mental health issues (Bomyea & Amir, 2011; Giancola, Shoal, & Mezzich, 2001; Jarrett, 2016).

The central executer's role allows humans to function within the confines of short-term working memory, as the short-term working memory serves as the "bottleneck" between the sensory register and long-term memory due to its capacity, form of storage, and duration of storage of information. In general, the capacity of short-term working memory is seven, plus or minus two units of information (Miller, 1956). Although the overall capacity of short-term working memory cannot be increased from seven informational units, the amount of information held *within* each unit can be increased through simple learning strategies such as chunking and mnemonic techniques (Rafoth, Leal, & DeFabo, 1993). Because of our reliance on language in everyday life, information within short-term working memory is stored largely in auditory form; and visual, spatial, and tactile forms of storing information have also been noted (Baddeley, 1986; 2001; Harris, Miniussi, Harris, & Diamond, 2002, Smith, 2000). Finally, short-term working memory stores information for the duration of five to 20 seconds before the effects of decay or interference become apparent (Peterson & Peterson, 1959).

Long-Term Memory

Long-term memory has been deemed the most complex component of the human memory system and it stores both declarative and procedural knowledge (Ormrod, 2008). Declarative knowledge refers to "how things are or were;" whereas procedural knowledge consists of "how to do things" (Ormrod, 2008, p. 182). The capacity, form of storage, and duration of information in long-term memory mirrors that of the sensory register and is less restrictive than the short-term working memory. As such, the capacity of long-term memory is unlimited and it contains explicit and implicit knowledge. Explicit knowledge consists of facts and details that are readily recalled and easily explained; whereas implicit knowledge affects our behavior and actions without our ability to consciously retrieve and explain it (Ormrod, 2008). Regardless of how the information is categorized, humans tend to remember the *gist* of information learned rather than word-for-word representations and detailed mental images. The information is then stored *semantically*, alongside of or within, concepts of similar meaning. The duration that information is stored in long-term memory is controversial, as some believe that once information is stored it remains there permanently and "forgetting" is a retrieval issue. Alternatively, others maintain that information in long-term memory can disappear based on how the information was originally stored and how often it is used (Ormrod, 2008). Thus overall, it is safest to assume that if properly encoded, information is stored in long-term memory for an indefinitely long period of time.

Transferring Information within the IPM

Knowing the capacity, form of storage, and duration of the IPM's components provides a context to better understand how information is transferred within the system. Information is transferred from the sensory-register to the short-term working memory largely through selective attention. In other words, we must attend to the information first in order for us to become conscious of it. Humans typically attend to information that stands-out because of its large size, intensity, novelty, motion, and incongruity within their context. We also are more likely to attend to information that is personally significant, has an emotional overtone, and is observed to be attended to by others (Barkley, 1996; Cowan, 1995; Kingstone, Smilek, Ristic, Friesen, & Eastwood, 2003; Sergeant, 1996).

Transferring information from short-term working memory to long-term memory is more complex, as it involves intentional processes on behalf of the learner. In essence, to be moved from short-term working memory to long-term memory, information needs to be organized, meaningful, and/or overlearned (Rafoth, Leal, & DeFabo, 1993). Organizing and making information meaningful occurs through elaboration techniques such as chunking, mnemonics, and visual/verbal elaboration—all of which are consciously superimposed on the information to be learned. Overlearning the material occurs through regular practice in retrieving the material and consistent self-testing. Consider the following examples. A student is charged with learning the capitals of the 50 states. The student will be most successful if he/she organizes the states according to geographic location (Northeast, Southeast, Midwest, Northwest, Southwest), notes the states visited, and draws a personally relevant picture of the state and its capital. In this example, the student has made the information meaningful through imposing an organization strategy (location) and invoking personal relevance through creating a picture of the state and capital and noting which states have been visited. Another example addresses our driving skills. When we first learn to drive, we are highly attentive to our surroundings and performance of the vehicle in relation to our commands, as we focus our attention on the road and our ability to keep the automobile in between the lines. After driving every day for ten years, the task has become overlearned and we consciously "think" while driving only when it is required due to changes in conditions of the automobile or roads.

As the ultimate goal of reading is to comprehend information, the ultimate goal of learning is to effectively and efficiently encode information in the short-term working memory so that it can be retrieved at a later time from long-term memory. Taken a step further, the goal is to overlearn the information so that we can perform the related task automatically. When tasks are performed automatically, they consume less space in our short-term working memory; thereby allowing sufficient room to simultaneously process additional stimuli and retrieve already existing information from long-term memory.

In summary, the Information Processing Model (IPM) is a widely researched and popular theory that is used to explain human learning. The IPM consists of the sensory-register, short-term working memory, and long-term memory and each of these components vary in the capacity, form, and duration of information stored. Information is moved through the IPM when it is consciously attended to, organized, and made meaningful to the learner. Short-term working memory is the lynchpin of the IPM, as it serves as the platform to conscious thought, "houses" the central executer, and bridges the sensory-register and long-term memory. Because short-term working memory has a limited capacity, it is easily overloaded by incoming stimuli that are unorganized and lack meaning. Information that is overlearned and effectively encoded consumes the least amount of storage space in short-term working memory; thus, allowing for a greater capacity to process additional stimuli and retrieve related information from long-term memory to facilitate more meaningful learning. With these conditions acknowledged, feedback of evaluation results to parents must be intentionally organized, void of frivolous details that may unnecessarily tax the capacity of parents' short-term working memory, and explicitly linked to the child's background information that is perceived to be meaningful by the parents. As such, conditions are created for parents to have the greatest likelihood to process the feedback content and correctly encode it in their long-term memory.

The IPM and Feedback Processes

Delivering feedback to parents occurs within the limitations of their short-term working memory. As described earlier, short-term working memory is essentially our consciousness and it allows us to process seven plus or minus two units of information within a 20-second duration. Thus theoretically, when parents arrive at the feedback meeting to learn of the evaluation results, they present with the full capacity (7 ± 2 units) to do so. However, the central executer and short-term working memory capacity have been noted to be adversely affected by anxiety, a characteristic that parents commonly cite to experience at the time of feedback (Bomyea & Amir, 2011; Engel, 1993; Giancola, Shoal, & Mezzich, 2001; Jarrett, 2016). Thus, when parents are feeling anxious at the time of feedback, they consciously experience this anxiety via their short-term working memory; thereby using some of the short-term working memory space to process the emotion. As such, parents' short-term working memory capacity is reduced from the onset and they attempt to process the content of the feedback meeting in the moment with already occurring limitations in their short-term working memory.

Given the condition of parents' short-term working memory at the time of feedback, clinicians must work to the greatest extent possible to reduce parent anxiety from the onset. One way to accomplish this task is through explicitly providing parents with an agenda at the beginning of the feedback meeting. Providing parents with an agenda at the start of the meeting has been recommended as an initial step in the feedback process (Tharinger, Finn, Hersh, Wilkinson, Christopher, & Tran, 2008). When presenting parents with this agenda, the clinician should explicitly emphasize the importance of active parent participation and briefly review: the purpose of the meeting, the length of time to complete the meeting, and an outline of how the meeting will be organized. Through utilizing an agenda, parents are better able to predict their immediate future and anticipate the "flow" of the feedback meeting; thereby reducing their anxiety and its adverse effects on their short-term working memory.

Another strategy to reduce parent anxiety and its adverse effects on short-term working memory during the feedback meeting consists of clinicians' language usage. Parent-professional communication is very complicated and asymmetry in communication almost always exists, as professionals talk differently to each other than to parents (Sands, 1988, 1994). Professionals speak in the "voice of science"; whereas, parents compose their thoughts from the "voice of the life world" (Sands, 1994). In general, the professional desires to be candid, clear, and thorough without unduly hurting the parents (Abrams & Goodman, 1998). Alternatively, the parents want to hear the truth but may resist it. Parents want professionals to listen to them and they have suggested that the feedback process emphasize recommendations, rather than assessment data (Abrams & Goodman, 1998; Cameron & Orr, 1991; Huebner, 1992; Silverstein, Springer, & Russo, 1992; Weill, 1999). Parents often describe professionals as insensitive and evasive; and parental dissatisfaction has been identified when professionals provide more directives and fewer client centered statements (Sands, 1994).

At the time of the feedback meeting parents desire to hear about their child's strengths, learn about the evaluation results through non-technical language, and to be linked with information resources (Huebner, 1992; Silverstein, Springer & Russo, 1992, Weill, 1999; Westling, 1997). The professional serves as an information resource when he or she discusses: medical conditions, physical characteristics of the child, how to teach a child at home, when and where to go for services, and the learning characteristics and potential of the child (Huebner, 1992; Silverstein, Springer, & Russo, 1992, Weill, 1999; Westling, 1997).

Clinicians elude speaking in the "voice of science" during feedback meetings when they make an intentional effort to avoid professional jargon. Previous research has emphasized the value of avoiding jargon, mirroring the parents' own language whenever possible, and utilizing metaphors that are familiar to the parents given their culture, occupation, and history (Glazer, 2014; Pollak, 1988; Tharinger, Finn, Hersh, Wilkinson, Christopher, & Tran, 2008). Through avoiding jargon and using familiar language, overloading parents' short-term working memory is circumvented, as parents do not need to use additional "space" in short-term working memory in attempting to decode the clinician's communication. Thus "room" is allotted in their short-term working memory for them to process feedback content and relate this content to information stored in their long-term memory. As a side note, avoiding jargon also helps to minimize parents' anxiety at the time of feedback. If parents do not understand the content of the feedback because of jargon, they are likely to become confused and this confusion leads to anxiety, which as described earlier, has adverse effects on parents' short-term working memory capacity.

Up to this point, much of the discussion regarding the IPM and feedback process has involved strategies to reduce parent anxiety as a means to increase parents' efficient and effective use of short-term working memory. You will later see these strategies embedded in the Feedback Model described in Chapter 6: *Creating a Permanent Product with the Parent: Utilizing the Feedback Model*. In addition to these strategies, you will notice that the Feedback Model requires the clinician to create a permanent product of the feedback results in the presence of the parent at the feedback meeting. Doing so individualizes the feedback content and intentionally provides parents with opportunity to actively participate in the feedback process. With these conditions, the feedback content becomes more personally relevant to the parents and it has a greater likelihood of being transferred to long-term memory for storage.

Summary

Chapter 3 provided an overview of the Information Processing Model and reviewed characteristics specific to the sensory register, short-term working memory, and long-term memory. Methods to transfer information among these components were discussed and limitations to the short-term working memory were highlighted while suggesting a rationale to recommendations for the feedback process that have been offered in the literature. In terms of the IPM, the ultimate goal of the feedback process is for parents to effectively code the feedback content in their short-term working memory so that it is transferred and stored in their long-term memory. Parental anxiety, jargon usage on behalf of the clinician, and unnecessary details within the feedback content impede this process and consume "space" in parents' short-term working memory that should otherwise be used to process the feedback results.

References

Abrams, E. Z., & Goodman, J. F. (1998). Diagnosing developmental problems in children: Parents and professionals negotiate bad news. *Journal of Pediatric Psychology, 23*(2), 87–98.

Atkinson, R. C., & Shiffrin, R. M. (1968). Human memory: A proposed system and its control processes. In K. W. Spence & J. T. Spence (Eds.), *The psychology of learning and motivation: Advances in research and theory* (Vol. 2). New York: Academic Press.

Atkinson, R. C., & Shiffrin, R. M. (1971). The control of short-term memory. *Scientific American, 225*, 2, 82–90.

Baddeley, A. D. (1986). *Working memory*. Oxford, England: Clarendon Press.

Baddeley, A. D. (2001). Is working memory still working? *American Psychologist, 56*, 851–864.

Barkley, R. A. (1996). Critical issues in research on attention. In G. R. Lyon & N. A. Krasnegor (Eds.), *Attention, memory, and executive function*. Baltimore, MD: Brookes.

Bomyea, J., & Amir, N. (2011). The effect of an executive functioning training program on working memory capacity and intrusive thoughts. *Cognitive Therapy Research, 35*, 529–535.

Cameron, S. J., & Orr, R. R. (1991). Parents' perceptions of professionals when their child has a developmental disability. *Guidance and Counseling, 6*(5), 43–50.

Cowan, N. (1995). *Attention and memory: An integrated framework*. New York: Oxford University Press.

Darwin, C. J., Turvey, M. T., & Crowder, R. G. (1972). An auditory analogue of the Sperling partial report procedure: Evidence for brief auditory storage. *Cognitive Psychology, 3*, 255–267.

Demetriou, A., Christou, C., Spanoudis, G., & Platsidou, M. (2002). The development of mental processing: Efficiency, working memory, and thinking. *Monographs of the Society for Research in Child Development, 67* (1, Serial No. 268).

Engel, D. M. (1993). Origin myths: Narratives of authority, resistance, disability and law. *Law and Society Review, 27*, 785–827.

Giancola, P. R., Shoal, G. D., & Mezzich, A. C. (2001). Constructive thinking, executive functioning, antisocial behavior, and drug use involvement in adolescent females with a substance use disorder. *Experimental and Clinical Psychopharmacology, 9*, 215–227.

Glazer, A. (2014). Communication matters: Effective oral communication of evaluation results. *Communique, 42*(6). Retrieved from www.nasponline.org

Han, S. H., & Kim, M. S. (2004). Visual search does not remain efficient when executive working memory is working. *Psychological Science, 15*, 623–628.

Harris, J. A., Miniussi, C., Harris, I. M., & Diamond, M. E. (2002). Transient storage of a tactile memory trace in primary somatosensory cortex. *Journal of Neuroscience, 22*, 8720–8725.

Huebner, E. S. (1992). Leadership skills for school psychologists: Improving parental involvement in multi-disciplinary team interactions. In S. Christenson & J. Close Conoley (Eds.), *Home-school collaboration: Enhancing children's academic and social competence* (pp. 409–422). Bethesda, MD: National Association of School Psychologists.

Jarrett, M. A. (2016). Attention-deficit/hyperactivity disorder (ADHD) symptoms, anxiety symptoms, and executive functioning in emerging adults. *Psychological Assessment, 28*, 245–250.

Kingstone, A., Smilek, D., Ristic, J., Friesen, C. K., & Eastwood, J. D. (2003). Attention, researchers! It is time to take a look at the real world. *Current Directions in Psychological Science, 12*, 176–180.

Loftus, G. R., & Loftus, E. F. (1976). *Human memory: The processing of information*. New York: Wiley.

Miller, G. A. (1956). The magical number seven, plus or minus two: Some limits on our capacity for processing information. *Psychological Review, 63*, 81–97.

Ormrod, J. E. (2008). *Human learning* (5th ed.). Upper Saddle River, NJ: Pearson Education.

Peterson, L. R., & Peterson, M. J. (1959). Short-term retention of individual items. *Journal of Experimental Psychology, 58*, 193–198.

Pollak, J. M. (1988). The feedback process with parents in child and adolescent psychological assessment. *Psychology in the Schools, 25*, 143–153.

Rafoth, M. A., Leal, L., & DeFabo, L. (1993). *Strategies for learning and remembering. Study skills across the curriculum*. National Education Association of the United States.

Sands, R. G. (1988). Sociolinguistic analysis of a mental health interview. *Social Work, 33,* 149–154.

Sands, R. G. (1994). A comparison of interprofessional and team-parent talk of an interdisciplinary team. *Social Work in Education, 16*(4), 207–220.

Sergeant, J. (1996). A theory of attention: An information processing perspective. In G. R. Lyon & N. A. Krasnegor (Eds.), *Attention, memory, and executive function* (pp. 57–69). Baltimore, MD: Brookes.

Silverstein, J., Springer, J., & Russo, N. (1992). Involving parents in the special education process. In S. Christenson & J. Close Conoley (Eds.), *Home-school collaboration: Enhancing children's academic and social competence* (pp. 383–408). Bethesda, MD: National Association of School Psychologists.

Smith, E. E. (2000). Neural bases of human working memory. *Current Directions in Psychological Science, 9,* 45–49.

Tharinger, D. J., Finn, S. E., Hersh, B., Wilkinson, A., Christopher, G. B., & Tran, A. (2008). Assessment feedback with parents and preadolescent children: A collaborative approach. *Professional Psychology: Research and Practice, 39*(6), 600–609.

Weill, M. (1999). Parent-teacher meetings: Dos and don'ts. In A. S. Cantor & S. A. Carroll (Eds.), *Helping children at home and school: Handouts from your school psychologist* (p. 79). Bethesda, MD: National Association of School Psychologists.

Westling, D. L. (1997). What parents of young children with mental disabilities want: The views of one community. *Focus on Autism and Other Developmental Disabilities, 12*(2), 67–80.

Willingham, D. T. (2004). *Cognition: The thinking animal* (2nd ed.). Upper Saddle River, NJ: Prentice Hall.

4 Parents and Special Education Meetings

Public education and the justice system seem to be the only venues wherein humans receive critical information affecting themselves or loved ones in the presence of an audience and they are expected to understand and accept this information which has life altering consequences. This chapter discusses parents' perceptions of special education meetings and stressors that may adversely influence the parents' ability to process feedback content given the inherent limitations of short-term working memory, as discussed in the previous chapter. Characteristics that may modulate parents' ability to understand and accept the evaluation results, such as their history of interaction with the public school, perceptions of self, and perceptions of the professional will be highlighted. Afterwards, the concepts of consumerism and anomie will be introduced to further help practitioners conceptualize parents' degree of need at the time of the feedback meeting. The chapter will conclude by discussing structural components of the Feedback Model that help to alleviate parents' degree of need at the feedback meeting.

As alluded to in previous chapters, a void seems to exist in literature that describes parent perceptions specific to feedback meetings; however, numerous studies have been published that describe parent perceptions of special education meetings and their reactions to having children with disabilities (Abrams & Goodman, 1998; Brinchmann, 1999; Burden & Thomas, 1986; Cameron & Orr, 1991; Crepeau, 2000; Engel, 1993; Fish, 1995; Jenson & Potter, 1990; Minke & Jenson, 2014; Pollak, 1988; Pruitt, Wandry, & Hollums, 1998). Some of these studies go beyond simply sharing parent testimonials and offer suggestions for practitioners to improve the content and process of special education meetings with parents (Cameron & Orr, 1991; Engel, 1993; Fish, 1995; Huebner, 1992; Lovitt, 1999; Margolis, 1998; Minke & Jenson, 2014; Pruitt, Wandry, & Hollums, 1998). Thus, the review of relevant literature in this area has been organized loosely into the five broad domains of: History, Communication, Characteristics of the Special Education Meeting, Parents' Perception of Self, and Parents' Perceptions of the Practitioner. These domains emerged in previous research as predictors of parental satisfaction following a multi-disciplinary evaluation for potential special education eligibility and they will be described in the following sections with the intent of sensitizing practitioners towards parental needs at the time of the feedback session (DeMatteo, 2005).

History

Research suggests that parents' history of interactions with educators and professionals affects satisfaction at the time of multi-disciplinary evaluation.Various authors have described parents as: 1) having negative past experiences when seeking services for themselves or family members, 2) receiving misinformation and/or unconfirmed information through media and neighborhood rumors, and 3) reflecting on negative memories of themselves as students (Cameron & Orr, 1991; Hayes, 1987; Seligman & Darling, 1997; Nowell & Salem, 2007; Silverstein, Springer, & Russo, 1992; Weill, 1999).

Negative Past Experiences with Service Providers

Past experiences with service providers on behalf of parents and family members seem to play an important role in influencing parent perceptions of the evaluation process.These past experiences appear to be unknowingly incorporated into the family belief system and they may later influence the manner in which other family members seek out and/or accept services and service providers.

According to researchers, parents seemed to be most defensive towards the special education evaluation process when their own mental health issues or those of family members were misdiagnosed in the past (Silverstein, Springer, & Russo, 1992). After a parent disorder is misdiagnosed by mental health providers in the private arena, the parent is likely to convey his or her distrust to the child. Because the child is exposed to this belief or attitude, the manner in which he or she might interact with a school psychologist or service provider becomes biased; thus, in turn adversely affecting potential evaluation results (Silverstein, Springer, & Russo, 1992).

Parents also attribute negative past experiences with service providers to professional insensitivity during communication of diagnosis and suspicions that the practitioner is withholding information (Cameron & Orr, 1991; Nowell & Salem, 2007; Seligman & Darling, 1997). Numerous testimonials cite the anger which parents experience after hearing a practitioner describe their child's disability in a manner which was perceived to be derogatory (Cameron & Orr, 1991; Sands, 1994; Seligman & Darling, 1997). According to some parents, the practitioner portrays the child as a "monster" when delivering the diagnosis (Cameron & Orr, 1991). In contrast, parents have become suspicious of practitioners when a disability is suspected, yet the possibility of its existence is not sufficiently explored, or it remains undiagnosed (Cameron & Orr, 1991; Seligman & Darling, 1997). From the parent's perspective, practitioners seem to lose credibility when they disregard parental observations of the child and neglect to somehow identify the significance of the reported problem (Cameron & Orr, 1991, Seligman & Darling, 1997).After the practitioner triggers parents' suspicions and/or is deemed to be insensitive, parents have been noted to typically change service providers and harbor feelings of discomfort and distrust towards the practitioner's service (Cameron & Orr, 1991).

Parents Receiving Misinformation—Rumors

The media serves as a powerful information tool for today's society. However, if parents' media exposure occurs without the proper guidance and prerequisite knowledge, the media may potentially contaminate parents' beliefs about service providers and individuals with disabilities. According to interview data gathered by researchers, parents typically form impressions about disabilities and service providers based on information obtained from talk shows, movies, and newspaper articles (Silverstein, Springer, & Russo, 1992). Although some information communicated through these methods may be helpful in identifying characteristics of a rare disorder and/or a unique treatment, media presentations have often been deemed as misleading to parents. Because of the misinformation parents obtain through the media, future understanding or acceptance of a particular disability or practitioner may be compromised (Silverstein, Springer, & Russo, 1992).

Similar to the media, gossip or rumors within a community play a powerful role in shaping parent perceptions about disabilities and service providers. When asked about what may have influenced their initial approach to the special education team, parents often cited the conversations that had occurred with other parents (Silverstein, Springer, & Russo, 1992). These conversations led to both positive and negative results during the parents' initial interaction with special education teams. For example, parents who have heard largely negative comments from others, may lower their expectations and approach the team with the intent of compromising (Silverstein, Springer, & Russo, 1992). Because this strategy causes them to "meet the team halfway," positive experiences have been noted to result (Silverstein, Springer, & Russo, 1992). In comparison, negative rumors have caused parents to approach teams defensively; thus, in turn, ultimately facilitating the conditions for contentious relationships.

Parents Reflecting on Negative Memories of Themselves as Students

Parents were also students at one point in their lives and they likely have a battery of positive and negative experiences that they reflect upon when considering their educational background. When remembering these experiences, parents recall their memories in an age specific manner related to the time during which they were stored (Hayes, 1987). For example, adults recall a particular high school experience through the perspective of an adolescent (Hayes, 1987). Because of this phenomenon, memories that adults may have acquired as students might be biased and are not necessarily accurate historical accounts (Hayes, 1987). Regardless, parents' memories of their educational experiences have an influence on their perceptions of teachers and service providers at the current time (Miller & Kraft, 2014; Seligman & Darling, 1997; Sheridan, Clarke, & Christenson, 2014). Silverstein, Springer, and Russo (1992) provide a brief example about a parent who was reluctant to complain about her treatment from school personnel. This parent's reluctance was attributed to a memory of herself as a student observing teachers comment negatively about a parent who "made waves" within the district

(Silverstein, Springer, & Russo, 1992). In this example, the parent's memory of a seemingly unrelated past experience influenced her perceptions about school personnel well into the future.

Throughout the literature reviewed, the influence of negative experiences in parents' history with service providers was largely emphasized. However, characteristics that seem to have led to positive future interactions between parents and professionals were also noted. For example, parents with the most positive early interactions reported their practitioner to be empathetic towards the needs of their child and family (Cameron & Orr, 1991). Additionally, early egalitarian relationships with professionals led to more positive future interactions (Silverstein, Springer, & Russo, 1992). This information supports the need for collaboration to occur at the time services are initially sought by parents.

Communication

Throughout literature reviewed, communication practices emerged to be an essential factor when exploring parent perceptions of special education meetings, as verbal communication is inevitably the primary medium through which information is transferred between parents and educational professionals. Within the following section, characteristics of parent-professional communication will be highlighted and the communicative asymmetry that exists between both parties will be explained. Afterwards, recommendations to improve communication on behalf of the practitioner will be discussed. The information reviewed has been obtained from literature in school psychology, social work, and health care professions.

Characteristics of Parent-Professional Communication

Because of the dynamics that occur during special education team meetings and the roles of the individuals involved, the communication characteristics of parents and practitioners inherently differ in three broad areas. These areas consist of: 1) the fundamental perspectives of the parent and professional, 2) the applicability of evaluation results in terms of time, and 3) differences in beliefs regarding the manner in which evaluation results are discussed.

First, as briefly described in Chapter 3, parents and professionals share information from fundamentally different perspectives during an evaluation. Parents have been deemed to speak in the voice of the "real world" and the data they contribute to the evaluation are obtained from the context of everyday life (Minke & Jenson, 2014; Sands, 1994). Parents may not have the formal training of professionals; however, they pride themselves in understanding how their child functions in practical situations (Pruitt, Wandry, & Hollums, 1998). In comparison, practitioners speak from the "voice of science" and they typically focus on diagnosis and norm referenced comparisons (Sands, 1994). Consequently, when professionals present feedback from an evaluation, they often over discuss assessment results and neglect to relate them to the constraints of the child's everyday life circumstances (Huebner, 1992; Seligman & Darling, 1997). Thus, practitioners have been criticized by parents for the disconnect that occurs between the evaluation results and the child's "true" levels of functioning, as observed in natural settings.

Next, parents and practitioners also differ in their perspectives regarding the applicability of evaluation results in terms of time. When an evaluation is pursued, parents are often frustrated and in a state of desperation, as they search for answers to their child's disability (Darling, 2003). Given these stressors, parents are primarily concerned with how the evaluation results affect the immediate life circumstances of their child (Westling, 1997). Questions such as, "Does my child have a particular disability?" or "Will he/she qualify for services at this time?" are often at the fore-front of the parent's stream of consciousness. Despite parents' sense of immediacy, professionals often present evaluation results with a focus on the future; and broad generalizations about anticipated levels of functioning are typically offered (Darling, 1997; Westling, 1997). This practice seems beneficial, as it is more global and introduces parents to issues that they may need to confront in the future. However, the practice has been suggested to be counterproductive because it overburdens parents' coping resources early during the identification phase (Darling, 1997).

Finally, parents and professionals seem to differ in their beliefs about the manner in which evaluation results are discussed. Following an evaluation, parents have been dissatisfied with the feedback that they received because they believed that the practitioner did not fully describe the evaluation results to them (Abrams & Goodman, 1998). Consequently, practitioners have been perceived as being evasive and their practices have been thought to inhibit parents from learning the "truth" about their child (Abrams & Goodman, 1998). Although parents may desire to hear the "truth" about their child, they often become resistant when the "truth" is presented (Abrams & Goodman, 1998). This behavior of the parents is then magni-fied when the diagnosis is uncertain and/or the nature of the disability is difficult to describe (Abrams & Goodman, 1998). In contrast, professionals have argued that they intentionally avoid delivering negative information to parents in an attempt to avoid parent self-blame and facilitate further discussion with themselves and/ or other service providers at future occasions (Merker, Hanson, & Poston, 2010; Sands, 1994).

The difference between parent and professional beliefs about the manner in which evaluation results are discussed seems attributable to the concept of asymmetry (Sands, 1988; 1994). Conversational asymmetry has been explored in sociolinguistic research wherein the verbal interactions between parents and professionals have been audio taped and later analyzed for linguistic idiosyncrasies specific to participants in a given conversation (Sands, 1994). Subsequent results have suggested that when a status difference exists among participants in a con-versation, language usage between both parties is less similar (Sands, 1994). Thus, misunderstandings and misperceptions of the intended message may likely result, especially by the participants with less developed linguistic skills (Lakoff, 1990; Sands, 1994). Because of asymmetry, conversations between professionals have been found to be qualitatively different than conversations between parents and professionals (Sands, 1988, 1994). In other words, professionals talk differently to each other than they do with parents (Sands, 1988, 1994). Thus, it is not surprising that when parents are professionals themselves, a fuller explanation of evaluation results have been noted to occur (Sands, 1994). These findings offer insight to the communication differences that exist between parents and practitioners at the time of the feedback session, as inequities of social status and linguistic facility seem innate to parent-professional communication.

How Parents Prefer Professionals to Communicate

A considerable amount of literature has been published that describes best practices when communicating with parents during special education team meetings (Diliberto & Brewer, 2014; Elizalde-Utnick, 2002; Fish, 1995; Flanagan, 2011; Glazer, 2014; Jenson & Potter, 1990; Kroth, 1985; Minke & Jenson, 2014; Pollack, 1988; Turnbull & Turnbull, 1986). Overall, parents desire practitioners to communicate in a non-technical language, avoid blame, and highlight the strengths, rather than weaknesses of the child (Hubbard & Adams, 2002; Huebner, 1992; Minke & Jenson, 2014; Phillips, 2008; Silverstein, Springer, & Russo, 1992; Weill, 1999). Educators and professionals are also described positively when they voice an awareness of the child's unique needs and cite roles the child may have outside of the specific disability (Darling, 1988; Lovitt, 1999; Tharinger, Finn, Hersh, Wilkinson, Christopher, & Tran, 2008; Weill, 1999).

At the time of meeting with the professionals, parents have described themselves to be most comfortable when practitioners explicitly ask them to: 1) share concerns about their child and his or her educational program, 2) provide information about the child's behavior at home, and 3) supply feedback in relation to the child's needs (Cameron & Orr, 1991; Huebner, 1992; Spann, Kohler, & Soenksen, 2003). In return, parents expressed an interest in learning from the practitioner more information regarding their child's levels of daily functioning, medical conditions, physical characteristics, and learning potential (Glazer, 2014; Pruitt, Wandry, & Hollums, 1998; Westling, 1997).

Furthermore, research has consistently stated that parents desire professionals who listen (Darling, 1997; Huebner, 1992; Kroth, 1985; Pruitt, Wandry, & Hollums, 1998; Silverstein, Springer, & Russo, 1992).

Physical Environment of the Meeting

Although a direct link has not yet been established, the physical environment where the feedback session occurs has the potential of influencing parents' behavior towards others in attendance. Studies exploring patient satisfaction outcomes within the health care profession have included items that ask the respondent to rate the "pleasantness" of the physical surroundings where the service is provided (Steiber & Krowinski, 1990). Literature in the mental health arena has also recommended that service providers target characteristics of the physical surroundings to improve upon reported client satisfaction (Stallard, 2001). Thus, the importance of physical environment has already begun to be explored in other service-oriented fields.

As applied to education, research has suggested that the physical and organizational structure of school buildings modulate the collaborative process with parents (Elizalde-Utnick, 2002; Sheridan, Clarke, & Christenson, 2014). Educational institutions that strive to improve home-school relationships have been recommended to create a warm welcoming atmosphere for parents and the community (Elizalde-Utnick, 2002; Swap, 1992). This recommendation seems especially applicable to special education team meetings.

Recommendations regarding the physical environment that may lead to improved outcomes of special education meetings are simple and almost common sense. The majority of recommendations can be easily adopted by educational professionals. However, it is acknowledged that the recommendations may be difficult to implement in some school buildings because of their outdated structures and limited resources. Overall, to improve upon the "pleasantness" of the feedback session, the meeting must be held in a setting that facilitates formal, friendly adult interaction (Swap, 1992; Minke & Jenson, 2014). Comfort, adult-sized chairs, and privacy are necessities; and light refreshments have been noted to add an additional welcoming touch (Swap, 1992; Eller, 2004). However, professionals have been recommended to refrain from eating or drinking if refreshments are not provided to the parents (Weill, 1999).

Characteristics of the Meeting

Special education team meetings with parents present with a set of qualitative characteristics in-and-of themselves. These characteristics establish the essence of the meeting, as a meeting does not exist without the presence of people and the review of assessment results within a given time period. Therefore, the following discussion will focus on research-based recommendations regarding: 1) organization of content, 2) time, and 3) the number of people present.

Organization of Content

Following a psycho-educational evaluation for potential special education eligibility, the ultimate goal of the team meeting is to provide an opportunity for information sharing between parents and professionals (Swap, 1992). To achieve this goal, practitioners must be proactive and become better oriented to the process of the special education team meetings, as effective meetings consist of components other than a simple face-to-face interaction. Researchers have recommended that professionals provide parents with a tentative agenda at the beginning of meetings (Diliberto & Brewer, 2014; Huebner, 1992; Minke & Jenson, 2014; Silverstein, Springer, & Russo, 1992; Swap, 1992; Tharinger, Finn, Hersh, Wilkinson, Christopher, & Tran, 2008). An agenda helps parents establish realistic expectations of the meeting and creates a framework for them to interpret information more accurately (Silverstein, Springer, & Russo, 1992). Thus, parents are more capable of asking relevant questions and digesting assessment results more comfortably, as they can anticipate topics of discussion and are less likely to feel overburdened with details (Silverstein, Springer, & Russo, 1992).

Literature has also recommended that parents be provided with a written description of instruments utilized during the evaluation (Pollak, 1988). This documentation can serve as a reference for parents at a later time when they might more comprehensively review the results. More importantly, it may lessen the need for parents becoming preoccupied with understanding specifics of the assessment instruments used throughout the evaluation thereby providing them with greater opportunities to be more active participants during the meeting.

Time

Depending on the circumstances, the overall length of the special education team meeting must be appropriate (Silverstein, Springer, & Russo, 1992; Swap, 1992; Minke & Jenson, 2014). In various studies, special education team meetings have averaged in length from 31 minutes to one hour, with researchers noting that meetings are typically brief given the complexity of the tasks that must be accomplished (Silverstein, Springer, & Russo, 1992; Ysseldyke, Algozzine, & Mitchell, 1982). These tasks include feedback of the assessment results, classification of special education eligibility, and IEP development (Silverstein, Springer, & Russo, 1992). Because lengthy meetings typically cause fatigue on behalf of the participants and brief meetings are characterized by superficial interactions, it has been recommended that meetings be divided into two sessions (Silverstein, Springer, & Russo, 1992). The first session for feedback of results and discussion of special education eligibility, and the second session dedicated to IEP development, if necessary (Silverstein, Springer, & Russo, 1992). As summarized and referenced best in Vickers, Minke, and Anderson's (2002) article, professionals are reminded: "In what other circumstance would one allow only 15 minutes to share a significant amount of information about a situation of deep mutual concern with a virtual stranger?" (p. 431).

From parents' perspective, longer special education team meetings are not necessarily required (Silverstein, Springer, & Russo, 1992). However, parents want more time with individual professionals throughout the special education determination and planning processes (Silverstein, Springer, & Russo, 1992). Parents seem to be searching for quality, rather than quantity in terms of time. To provide greater opportunity for questions and discussion of recommendations, professionals have been recommended to organize feedback results around a specific time limit to maintain efficiency and limit fatigue on behalf of all parties involved (Pollak, 1988).

Number of People Present

Federal regulations dictate those who are required to be present at special education eligibility determination meetings (Federal Register, 2006). At minimum, these meetings must consist of the child's parents, school psychologist, regular education teacher, special education teacher, and a representative of the public agency who is qualified to supervise the delivery of specially designed instruction to meet the child's needs. It may be necessary for additional participants with "specific expertise" to attend the meeting if requested by the parents and/or it is determined that the child presents with more extensive needs. Assuming that the child presents with relatively common needs, one might expect eligibility determination meetings to consist of approximately four to six participants.

Despite federal regulations, the number of participants in special education eligibility determination meetings seems to have increased. The special education team has been described as a "big machine" and it has been noted to have an inordinate number of participants given the circumstances (Engel, 1993). In such situations, parents' feelings of anxiety, intimidation, and fearfulness have been exacerbated; and the meaningfulness of the contributions from those present has been more regularly questioned (Engel, 1993; Shaver, 2015). Consider the following parent testimonials describing the team meeting. "It is a long, intimidating table where you're this tiny little dot at one end, and they're all sitting up there at the other end. And some of them are literally almost asleep, and they could care less that they're there" (Engel, 1993; p. 55). In another example, the parent provides a direct reference to the large number participants. "I get nervous when I'm with them, because it's 12 against 1 … when I go to that committee, I'm blown away. I mean, I've got to take a tranquilizer before I go" (Engel, 1993; p. 56). In both instances, the large number of participants on the special education team seems to have adversely influenced parents' perceptions of themselves and the practitioner. A best-practices approach would keep the meeting's attendance to the smallest number as possible (Margolis, 1998).

Parent Perceptions of Self

Research has generally described parent perceptions of self during special education team meetings to be less than favorable (Denman, 2014; Engel, 1993; Fish, 2008; Lovitt, 1999; Silverstein, Springer, & Russo, 1992). Although this negativity may be the outcome of the interaction among numerous variables, it is also possible that parent perceptions of self are linked to their lack of understanding of IDEA regulations. These regulations have forced parents into an active nontraditional role within an uncommon situation (Engel, 1993; Federal Register, 2006; Phillips, 2008). In turn, this role and their lack of understanding of the special education evaluation process thereby influences negative perceptions of themselves. Parent perceptions of self during special education team meetings will be described in the following section. Afterwards, the influence of IDEA regulations on parent perceptions will be highlighted and the concept of parent understanding will be reviewed.

Many parents have described special education team meetings unfavorably (Engel, 1993; Pruitt, Wandry, & Hollums, 1998; Lovitt, 1999; Phillips, 2008; Silverstein, Springer, & Russo, 1992; Spann, Kohler, & Soenksen, 2003). Parents have compared the team meeting to being judged by a committee within a courtroom (Engel, 1993). Parents have suspected that others have talked about them before the team meeting; and they have described the special education team as a "big machine" that will grind out decisions despite their input (Engel, 1993). As parents described the special education team in such a manner, feelings of intimidation, alienation, and confusion were emphasized (Engel, 1993; Lovitt, 1999; Phillips, 2008; Pruitt, Wandry, & Hollums, 1998; Silverstein, Springer, & Russo, 1992). In some cases, the intimidation was so overwhelming that parents intentionally restricted their degree of participation, even though team recommendations were against their beliefs (Engel, 1993). In other cases, parent participation was limited because of their fearfulness to admit their confusion, as they restrained themselves from asking questions in order to uphold their own credibility (Silverstein, Springer, & Russo, 1992). When considering how parents have characterized the special education team meeting and described perceptions of themselves, it appears that the interpersonal dynamics of special education teams may force parents into an inferior role. This role is ultimately believed to be counterproductive to the best interest of the student.

Researchers have emphatically argued that the primary goal of special education multi-disciplinary teams is to promote collaboration, or true partnerships, among team members (Christenson, 1995; Christenson, Rounds, & Franklin, 1992; Elizalde-Utnick, 2002; Fish, 1995; Miller & Kraft, 2014; Minke, 2000; Stanovich, 1996; Vickers, Minke, & Anderson, 2002). To accomplish this task, the CORE elements of the collaborative process must be present (Minke, 2000). In other words, team members must: 1) trust each other (Connect), 2) avoid blame (Optimistic), 3) accept others' expertise (Respect), and 4) believe that all participants are partners (Empowerment) (Minke, 2000). Underlying each of these elements is a theme of coequal status among team members for the purpose of problem solving (Minke, 2000). It is this theme of coequal status that seems to conflict with IDEA regulations and facilitate negative parent perceptions of self.

The special education process is dictated by IDEA regulations and it has been argued to parallel a medical model, as an unavoidable status difference between parents and other members of the special education team naturally exists (Engel, 1993; Phillips, 2008). In a sense, IDEA regulations have forced parents into believing that they have a "true" partnership with professionals (Engel, 1993; Federal Register, 2006). This belief might compel parents into a dilemma, as they remember past interactions with medical doctors and recall that they did not have an "equal say" in their treatment (Engel, 1993). Consequently, the parameters of the special education team meeting send parents a double message. As parents are anticipated to be coequals with professionals, they are expected to meaningfully contribute, or to have an understanding of the meeting. Yet, the majority of parents do not have the specialty training that leads to understanding, as do other team members. Furthermore, parents have been described to be unfamiliar with the special education process in terms of their ability to explain the process and outcome (Lovitt, 1999; Phillips, 2008). After parents recognize the discrepancy between the expectation to be proficient with special education and reality, feelings of inferiority and confusion may naturally result. These feelings conflict with previous information the parent may have received indicating that he or she is intended to be a coequal member of the team.

To circumvent feelings of confusion and inferiority and improve parent perceptions of self during the special education team meeting, it is necessary for parents to acquire an understanding of the special education process (Silverstein, Springer, & Russo, 1992; Phillips, 2008). More specifically, parents need to develop a more intense awareness of special education regulations, due process rights, classification systems, placement options, and school culture (Silverstein, Springer, &

Russo, 1992; Phillips, 2008). To accomplish this goal, researchers have recommended that the special education team: 1) provide parents with time to absorb the assessment results, 2) allow parents to observe parts of the assessment, 3) review the assessment data on which placement decisions were based, and 4) encourage questions while communicating in a "straight talk" manner (Silverstein, Springer, & Russo, 1992). Each of these recommendations seems to lessen the discrepancy between parents' perceptions and the goal of coequal status, as their likelihood of understanding the process and the roles of the other team members increases.

Parent Perceptions of the Professional

Parents have generally perceived professionals as having subject knowledge in their area of expertise, but a limited understanding of their child as an individual (Engel, 1993; Lovitt, 1999; Nowell & Salem, 2007; Pruitt, Wandry, & Hollums, 1998). This parent perception seems to be the partial byproduct of the primary dynamic that occurs during special education team meetings, as dictated by IDEA regulations (Federal Register, 2006). Therefore, the following section will: 1) describe parent perceptions of the professional, 2) offer an explanation of those perceptions by reflecting on the special education model, and 3) highlight parent report of perceived positive characteristics of professionals.

Parent perceptions of professionals seem paradoxical. According to testimonials, parents have identified professionals to be powerful, they have reported to be "in awe" of professional knowledge, and they have identified the professional as the expert (Denman, 2014; Sands, 1994; Seligman & Darling, 1997; Silverstein, Springer, & Russo, 1992). From the parents' perspective, information communicated by professionals during team meetings has been identified to be of great importance; and subsequent conclusions from professionals have been reported to be definitive (Sands, 1994). Despite these beliefs that suggest infallibility, parents have stated that professionals generally know very little about their children and they are reluctant to recognize the family's perspective during educational decision making (Engel, 1993; Lovitt, 1999; Nowell & Salem, 2007; Pruitt, Wandry, & Hollums, 1998). Overall, parent reports have suggested that a considerable degree of professional dominance continues to exist; although, some sources noted that it has been slowly decreasing (Seligman & Darling, 1997). Regardless, it seems likely that professional dominance will remain evident until the structural model of special education dramatically changes (Phillips, 2008).

Such parental perceptions of professionals are expected to some degree, given the dynamics of the special education team meeting and the model of eligibility determination and service delivery. In his encompassing article to describe perceptions of "rights" and "needs" of individuals with difficulties, Rappaport (1981) defines the concepts of prevention and empowerment as service delivery options. A prevention model views people as children; and it has been derived from the needs of dependent people (Rappaport, 1981). Professional experts are essential to prevention, as prevention implies that experts fix independent variables to achieve an appropriate outcome on the dependent variable (Rappaport, 1981). In comparison, an empowerment model posits that poor functioning results from social structure and lack of resources that make it impossible for competencies to operate (Dunst, Trivette, & Deal, 1994; Rappaport, 1981). Empowerment naturally promotes collaboration and it "enhances the possibilities for people to control their own lives" (Rappaport, 1981; p. 15).

Based on the information offered by Rappaport (1981), special education team meetings seem to be best described by the prevention model. As emphasized throughout federal regulations, the identification, evaluation, and placement of children with suspected disabilities is to be driven by documented needs (Federal Register, 2006). Furthermore, it is implied that the Individual Education Plan (IEP) is a treatment designed to ultimately improve the child's academic success. These themes suggest that special education regulations foster a dependency between parents and professionals. This dependency reinforces the status difference; thereby affecting the roles that each adopt in the multi-disciplinary team meeting, which in turn affects perceptions.

Research has reported positive characteristics of professionals cited by parents (Cameron & Orr, 1991; Pruitt, Wandry, & Hollums, 1998; Seligman & Darling, 1997; Silverstein, Springer, & Russo, 1992). Parents have described an effective professional as one who is not an expert, but demonstrates a "professional aura" (Silverstein, Springer, & Russo, 1992). A desire for the professional to treat parents as they would a friend was noted; and respect and empathy for the child's needs and family were described to be critical (Cameron & Orr, 1991; Pruitt, Wandry, & Hollums, 1998). Additionally, professionals must embrace realistic role expectations for the parent (Seligman & Darling, 1997). These expectations need to be compatible with parent perceptions of self to facilitate receptiveness during feedback and adherence to recommendations (Seligman & Darling, 1997; Tharinger, Finn, Hersh, Wilkinson, & Tran, 2008). Professionals who demonstrate these characteristics are likely to be positively perceived by parents; thus, ultimately increasing the chances of amicable special education team meetings in the future.

To summarize, parents' perceptions of professionals are complex and interdependent on a multitude of factors, many of which are beyond the scope of this text to discuss. These perceptions seem to be indirectly influenced by special education regulations. The special education regulations may very well foster a dependent relationship between service provider and recipient while also dictating the role of special education team members. In many cases parent perceptions appear incongruent, as parents seem to value professional characteristics that might not necessarily be considered "professional" by the practitioner. As examples, practitioners might feel uncomfortable treating parents as they would a friend and their respect and empathy towards the parent and family may be overshadowed by the magnitude of the child's needs identified by the evaluation.

Addressing Parents' Degree of Need: Consumerism and Anomie

Simply stated, parents' behavior at the time of the feedback meeting is a product of an interaction among a multitude of factors that can be linked to their history of educational experiences, the physical environment where the meeting occurs, the nature of communication during the meeting, perceptions of self, and their perceptions of the professional. With these factors, parents may demonstrate a considerable degree of need at the time of the feedback meeting, as literature has documented the paradoxical nature of the parent-practitioner relationship in terms of expectations and perceptions (Pruitt, Wandry, & Hollums, 1998; Darling, 1988; Valle, 2011). Essentially, parents desire professionals to: 1) satisfy their emotional needs, 2) take a personal interest in their child, 3) treat their child as a unique individual, and 4) consider roles the child has other than the disability including those of a son, sibling, playmate, and student (Darling, 1988). In contrast, professionals: 1) typically remain affectively neutral, 2) often focus on the child's disability and weaknesses rather than strengths, and 3) unknowingly communicate that all cases are similar instead of unique (Darling, 1988). At its most simple level, this paradox between parents and professionals seems to be the product of historical struggles between both groups; and it will likely continue to exist until expectations and perceptions of both parties assimilate.

Parents as Consumers: A Growing Trend in Special Education

Parent and professional roles in Special Education have followed the ebb and flow of science and historical consequences between the two entities. As parents historically sought services for children with disabilities, professionals typically responded by becoming more involved; and as professionals became more involved, parents seemed to retreat and adopt a passive role (Phillips, 2008). Thus, a constant flux appears to have traditionally existed between the two groups. In the following section, consumerism will be introduced as a business-related topic and then discussed with reflection on mental health and education disciplines. Afterwards, an underlying rationale to consumerism will be presented and a prescription to address parents with significant needs as customers will be offered.

Consumerism has traditionally been at the nexus of business-related fields, as it has served as a force to ensure the production of quality products and satisfaction of customers. Within business, if a product does not meet a customer's needs, the customer will buy another product, shop elsewhere, or not shop at all. This parameter seems easy to comprehend when a concrete entity is involved. However, when the product the customer seeks becomes more abstract in nature, as with a service, the degree to which the product meets the customer's needs becomes subjective and judgmental, as perceptions become involved.

Especially damaging to perceptions is information obtained from what seems to be professional sources; information that is often not understood in the correct context. As society matures, communication mediums improve, and technological advances occur, individuals have access to information and knowledge in virtually any topic area. This access to information can be extremely beneficial and empowering, as it provides one the ability to better identify resources and opportunities to improve one's circumstances. However, without the proper interpretation and prerequisite awareness, easy access to information and knowledge may provide some with self-perceptions that they are proficient in a particular area. Unbeknownst to these individuals, this proficiency is superficial in nature, and to a large degree, it cannot substitute for professional training and experience in a particular field.

As recipients of services and those who speak on their behalf perceive themselves to be more knowledgeable, they adopt a role that allows them to monitor and question the services they receive from health care and education. As a result, literature has identified these individuals as consumers (Darling, 1988; Denman, 2014; Pruitt, Wandry, & Hollums, 1998; Salisbury & Branson, 1997; Sands, 1994; Stallard, 1996). Consider the following examples. Darling (1988) has provided a detailed description of the evolution of consumerism among parents of individuals with disabilities; and parents have been characterized as consumers in research that documented parental expectations of special educators within a community (Pruitt, Wandry, & Hollums, 1998; Valle, 2011). Service recipients have also been stated to be consumers in literature addressing satisfaction measures within education and mental health related fields (Stallard, 1996). Consumerism has been cited in a study that investigated communication patterns during interdisciplinary team meetings with parents (Sands, 1994). Thus, consumerism has been referred to in a variety of research studies that have centered around addressing the needs of others in a public service-oriented manner. It can be assumed that these needs exist on a continuum. Customers with minimal needs are likely to be content with ordinary services offered within a given setting. In comparison, individuals with greater needs may require additional efforts by the service provider to shape the perceived needs in a manner that can be sufficiently addressed by the resources within the particular setting.

To understand needs of parents as consumers, it is necessary to acknowledge parent perceptions and expectations of themselves and their children. Prior to the birth of their child, parents develop perceptions about parenting and expectations regarding their children (Seligman & Darling, 1997). These perceptions and expectations surround the idea of normalization and serve as a template for future reference (Darling, 2003; Seligman & Darling, 1997). In other words, parents envision having adequate housing for their family, sufficient resources to maintain a reasonable lifestyle, and some degree of leisure time to pursue other interests (Darling, 2003). Furthermore, parents expect to have a normal baby who grows to become a contributing member of society and experiences academic, social, and emotional success at a level equal to or above similar aged peers (Seligman & Darling, 1997). When parents learn of circumstances, such as a disability, which may threaten this idea of normalization, their template of family, parenting, and children becomes inconsistent with reality (Darling, 2003). As a result, parents stumble into a state of anomie (Darling, 1988, 2003).

Anomie has been defined as a state of normlessness and lack of definitional clarity (Darling, 2003, 1988). One who experiences anomie feels powerless and has difficulty giving meaning to a situation. Using a hypothetical example, anomie has been described as the overwhelming feeling one likely gets if he or she were to be unknowingly dropped in a strange location with unfamiliar language, customs, and beliefs (Darling, 2003). The experience of anomie typically compels parents into a seekership role, as they search for answers to explain their child's disability and struggle to create a new template of normalization (Darling, 2003;

Engel, 1993). Furthermore, this anomie seems to serve as a catalyst in intensifying the degree of need parents present to the service provider.

As a seeker, parents search for information, attempt to regain control, and challenge authority to secure educational services (Darling, 1988; 2003). This behavioral repertoire has been referred to as "entrepreneurial" in nature (Darling, 1988; 2003). Parents may visit numerous professionals for an "accurate" diagnosis and the suitability of educational services within the public school is questioned (Pruitt, Wandry, & Hollums, 1998; Westling, 1997; Valle, 2011). In response to these actions, potential service providers may perceive parents to be "difficult" and misinterpret their degree of need as being malicious.

Parents who present with significant needs can be a source of great conflict for the school district and ultimately damage the well-being of the student with disabilities. As Lake (2000) notes, conflict between parents and schools weakens home-school relationships, causes stress for all parties involved, and drains financial resources through due process hearings and mediations. When including attorney fees, court transcripts, and staff time, conflict resolution has been cited to cost between \$5,000 to \$30,000, without considering the further possibility that the student may also be entitled to some form of compensatory education at the district's expense (Crowley, Smit, & David, 1991; Phillips, 2008). Given the magnitude of this information and the common belief that many schools are already lacking in resources, it becomes necessary for professionals to utilize practices that have the likelihood of reducing potential conflicts between home and school. Therefore, the anomie that parents may experience at the time of diagnosis and throughout the special education process must be considered and addressed by taking steps to reduce parent's degree of need.

Alleviating Parents' Degree of Need via the Feedback Model

The Feedback Model's design is rooted in literature regarding family-school collaboration, home-school meetings, and the Information Processing Model (IPM). As such, the Feedback Model inherently works to reduce parents' degree of need at the time of the feedback meeting through incorporating methods to structure the feedback meeting, guide communication, and improve upon parents' perceptions of self and the practitioner. Each of these methods will be reviewed in the following section and discussed with more detail in Chapters 5 and 6.

Structuring the Feedback Meeting

The Feedback Model utilizes a prescribed set of 16 steps that superimposes a developmental structure onto the feedback meeting. The first eight steps create the backdrop to the presentation of actual evaluation data in Steps 9 through 16. The model begins with the practitioner (1) "hosting" the parent. While hosting, the practitioner engages the parent in "neutral" conversation to build or reestablish rapport. Afterwards, the practitioner (2) explicitly identifies one unique attribute of the child to communicate to the parent an awareness of the child's humanness and individuality, rather than perceiving the child as "another case number." Next, the practitioner (3) asks the parent to comment on how the child perceived the evaluation process. The purpose of this step is to give the parent an opportunity to talk while the practitioner obtains data to help gauge the parent's potential resistance to the evaluation results. Following the parent's response, the practitioner (4) states the purpose of the meeting. This step begins to establish the meeting agenda and communicates to the parent that he or she will be receiving information to assist with understanding the detailed and complex psycho-educational report. In the next step (5) the practitioner offers a broad overview of the evaluation process and shares a more detailed agenda. This step reminds the parent of the multi-modal and multi-factor nature of the evaluation and his or her participation in the process. Afterwards, the practitioner (6) delivers a brief overview of standardized assessment to inform the parent that the results are discussed in terms of ranges rather than the percent-correct metric commonly used in classroom exams. Upon sharing this information, the practitioner then begins to (7) draw a horizontal line graph, labeling the left margin with the categories of ranges while explaining what performance in each range entails. In doing so, the practitioner creates a permanent product in the parent's presence; thereby communicating the practitioner's operational understanding of the evaluation and knowledge of the child as an individual. Following creation of the graph and explanation of ranges, the practitioner (8) explains caveats to score ranges and interpretations; thus, promoting transparency and providing the parent with the basic tools to understand intra and inter individual differences of the child's performance before the actual performance is graphed.

After creating the graph and explaining caveats to score ranges and interpretations, the practitioner (9) explains and draws the factor structure of the cognitive instrument on the reverse side of the graph and then (10) plots the overall cognitive score and factor scores on the graph. With the parent already having knowledge of the range categories, he or she *sees* where his or her child performed before *hearing* of the results; thus making abstract information concrete. Steps 9 and 10 are then applied to the academic achievement measure and repeated for Steps 11 and 12. Afterwards, performance on the curriculum-based measure (13) is verbally described while relating the results to the academic achievement data plots on the graph. Visual-motor functioning (14) and broad behavioral ratings (15) are then plotted before proceeding to conclusions and recommendations (16) where the rationale to eligibility determination and recommendations for programming are then shared.

Guiding Communication

The Feedback Model incorporates specific verbiage at each step that helps to guide communication during the feedback session. This verbiage intentionally has a "real-world" tone to avoid the risk of conversational asymmetry occurring between parent and practitioner, as described earlier. The verbiage also intentionally utilizes the pronoun *we* to emphasize the collaborative nature of the feedback session and remind the parent that he or she is a member of the evaluation team who participated in the evaluation process through completing rating scales and/

or sharing interview and observation data. Practitioners are recommended to use the pronoun *we* rather than *I* to avoid unintentionally making the evaluation about them instead of the student and leading the parents to believe that the results are due to the practitioner rather than the student.

Consider the following verbiage included in the Feedback Model. In Step 4 when sharing the purpose of the feedback session the practitioner states the following, "The purpose of this meeting is for us to review a 'snapshot' of [child's name] performance on the evaluation. You will receive [or already have] a detailed report that you can read at your leisure."

Similarly, in Step 5 when providing an overview of the evaluation and establishing an agenda, the practitioner states:

> During the time with [child's name], we measured how smart he is; his academic skills in reading, written language, oral language, and math; his visual-motor functioning, collected behavioral ratings from [student's name], you, and his teacher; and made some general observations. The goal of this process is to take all of this information and sift through it, looking to see what types of recommendations it would lead to.

Likewise in Step 6 when providing an overview of standardized assessment the practitioner states:

> When we conduct formal evaluations on students, we compare [child's name] performance to others of similar age in the standardization sample. The standardization sample being a group of other similar aged kids in the United States that the instrument is based on. When we do this comparison, performance is classified in different ranges.

In addition to using the pronoun *we* in place of *I*, the Feedback Model utilizes parent-friendly language to explain constructs measured in the cognitive, academic, visual-motor, and behavioral domains. Doing so helps to avoid overloading the parent's short-term working memory capacity and allow adequate cognitive resources for the parent to process the information. Thus, the likelihood of parent confusion is reduced; and frustration and anomie are avoided. Consider the following examples that will be further discussed in Chapter 5.

When reviewing the cognitive instrument utilized in the evaluation, the practitioner avoids terms such as intelligence and cognitive functioning and instead describes the construct as "how smart [student's name] is." Similarly, in place of describing the student's academic functioning, the practitioner talks about "school related skills such as reading, written language, math, and oral language." The practitioner explains visual-motor skills as "the ability to copy increasingly complex figures on paper" and behavioral functioning is broadly portrayed through language that illustrates the student's ability "to get-along-with-others in the home and school environments." In each of these instances, abstract language (i.e. cognitive functioning, academic skills) is replaced by concrete terminology that is more familiar to the parent.

Improving Parents' Perceptions of Self and the Practitioner

It is imperative that the feedback session actively programs to include techniques and strategies to improve upon parents' perceptions of self and the professional at the time of meeting. Parents who distrust the practitioner and feel alienated and confused are at risk of entering a state of anomie and adopting a seeker-ship role; both of which impede their acceptance of the evaluation results and ultimately affect the overall adjustment of the child. As such, the Feedback Model is intentionally designed to promote transparency of the evaluation process and empower parents to be active participants in the decision-making process regarding their child. Both of these characteristics in-and-of-themselves should help precipitate improved parent perceptions of self and the practitioner at the time of the feedback session, as the parent is regarded as a co-equal member of the evaluation team.

To further support parents' active participation in the feedback meeting, the Feedback Model requires practitioners to create a permanent product of the child's evaluation results in the presence of the parent. In Steps 7 through 16, the practitioner draws out the graph, describes the descriptive ranges, explains the instruments, and then plots the child's performance in the presence of the parent. This practice is in direct contrast to simply providing the parent with a copy of the psycho-educational report or a printout of scores at the time of meeting—a practice that creates a hierarchy between the practitioner and parent and emphasizes the power differential. With the Feedback Model, the practitioner plots the child's performance *with* the parent during the feedback session. In essence, the parent then participates in creating the child's overall profile of performance on the evaluation; thereby nurturing his or her feelings of self-efficacy and improving upon the practitioner's credibility as perceived by the parent. With such experience, the parent then leaves the feedback session with a more positive perception of self and the practitioner; thus, reducing the likelihood of him or her adopting a seeker-ship role.

Summary

Chapter 4 provided an in-depth discussion of parents' perceptions of special education meetings and stressors that may adversely influence the parents' ability to process feedback content given the inherent limitations of short-term working memory. A literature review yielded six broad factors that may influence parents' ability to understand and accept the evaluation results—History, Communication, Physical Environment, Characteristics of the Meeting, Parent Perceptions of Self, and Parent Perceptions of the Professional.

In further dissection of these factors, we learn that parent reactions to the feedback meeting may be attributed to their history of interactions with mental health practitioners and memories of themselves as students. Conversational asymmetry is typically evident between parents and practitioners, as parents speak in the "voice of the real world" whereas practitioners speak in the "voice of science." Parents desire the practitioner to communicate in a non-technical language, avoid blame, highlight the child's strengths, and perceive the child as a unique individual rather than a case-number. A comfortable meeting environment may influence positive perceptions of the feedback meeting on behalf of the parent and presenting the parent with a meeting agenda beforehand helps to lower parent anxiety. A smaller number of people attending the feedback session may be beneficial, as parents have noted feelings of intimidation with large meetings; and parents yearn for quality time with individual practitioners rather than longer team meetings. In the end, parents desire a practitioner who is a "friendly expert" and has realistic role expectations of the parent.

Ignoring the literature and its recommendations can increase parents' susceptibility of experiencing anomie; thereby expanding their risk of adopting a seeker-ship role. Although the seeker-ship role has its benefits in helping parents normalize their child's circumstances within the context of the family, seeker-ship delays parents' acceptance of the evaluation results and may lead to considerable conflict with the school, which in turn fuels a future of intense home-school interactions. Thus, practitioners must utilize feedback practices that are research based and intentionally address parents' degree of need at the time of the feedback session.

The Feedback Model is rooted in literature focused on delivering evaluation results to parents and parents' interactions with the special education team. Specific content and process techniques of the Feedback Model are described in upcoming chapters, as it organizes the feedback session, tempers practitioners' communication, and encourages active parent participation. With these conditions fulfilled, the feedback process realizes its ultimate goal of providing parents with credible information to better understand their child and use during the decision-making process.

References

Abrams, E. Z., & Goodman, J. F. (1998). Diagnosing developmental problems in children: Parents and professionals negotiate bad news. *Journal of Pediatric Psychology, 23*(2), 87–98.

Brinchmann, B. S. (1999). When home becomes a prison: Living with a severely disabled child. *Nursing Ethics, 6*(2), 137–144.

Burden, R., & Thomas, D. (1986). A further perspective on parental reaction to handicap. *The Exceptional Child, 33*(2), 140–145.

Cameron, S. J., & Orr, R. R. (1991). Parents' perceptions of professionals when their child has a developmental disability. *Guidance and Counseling, 6*(5), 43–50.

Christenson, S. L. (1995). Best practices in supporting home-school collaboration. In A. Thomas & J. Grimes (Eds.), *Best practices in school psychology* (3rd ed., pp. 253–268). Bethesda, MD: National Association of School Psychologists.

Christenson, S. L., Rounds, T., & Franklin, M. J. (1992). Home-school collaboration: Effects, issues, and opportunities. In S. Christenson & J. Close Conoley (Eds.), *Home-school collaboration: Enhancing children's academic and social competence* (pp. 19–52) Bethesda, MD: National Association of School Psychologists.

Crepeau, E. B. (2000). Reconstructing gloria: A narrative analysis of team meetings. *Qualitative Health Research, 10*(6), 766–787.

Crowley, C., Smith, A., & David, T. (1991). Illinois mediation model assuages special education disputes. *National Institute for Dispute Resolution*, 16–19.

Darling, R. B. (1988). Parental entrepreneurship: A consumerist response to professional dominance. *Journal of Social Issues, 44*(1), 141–158.

Darling, R. B. (2003). Families of children with disabilities: *Reactions to diagnostic information and effects on family life.* Presentation at the Association of School Psychologists of Pennsylvania Spring Conference, Harrisburg, PA, March.

DeMatteo, F.J. (2005). *Predictors of parent satisfaction following multi-disciplinary evaluation for special education eligibility.* (Doctoral dissertation, Indiana University of Pennsylvania, 2005).

Denman, S.J. (2014). Parents as experts on children with disabilities: Being prepared for the long-haul. *International Journal of Disability, Development and Education, 61*(4), 434–440.

Diliberto, J.A. & Brewer, D. (2014). Six tips for successful IEP meetings. *Teaching Exceptional Children, 47*(2), 128–135.

Dunst, C. J., Trivette, C. M., & Deal, A. G. (Eds.). (1994). *Supporting and strengthening families.* Cambridge, MA: Brookline Books.

Elizalde-Utnick, G. (2002). Best practices in building partnerships with families. In A. Thomas & J. Grimes (Eds.), *Best practices in school psychology* (4th ed., pp. 413–429). Bethesda, MD: National Association of School Psychologists.

Eller, J. (2004). *Effective group facilitation in education: How to energize meetings and manage difficult groups.* Thousand Oaks, CA: Corwin.

Engel, D. M. (1993). Origin myths: Narratives of authority, resistance, disability, and law. *Law and Society Review, 27*(4), 785–827.

Federal Register (2006). *Part II. Department of Education: 34 CFR Parts 300 and 301. Assistance to states for the education of children with disabilities and preschool grants for children with disabilities; Final rule.* Retrieved from http://edocket.access.gpo.gov/2006/pdf/06-6656.pdf

Fish, M. C. (1995). Best practices in working with parents of children with disabilities. In A. Thomas & J. Grimes (Eds.), *Best practices in school psychology* (3rd ed., pp. 1061–1070). Bethesda, MD: National Association of School Psychologists.

Fish, W. W. (2008). The IEP meeting: Perceptions of parents of students who receive special education services. *Preventing School Failure, 53*, 8–14.

Flanagan, R. (2011). Parent feedback conferences: An opportunity to intervene. *Psychology in the Schools, 48*(3), 307–315.

Glazer, A. (2014). Communication matters: Effective oral communication of evaluation results. *Communique, 42*(6). Retrieved from www.nasponline.org

Hayes, R. L. (1987). The reconstruction of educational experience: The parent conference. *Education, 107*(3), 305–309.

Hubbard, D. D., & Adams, J. (2002). Best practices in facilitating meaningful family involvement in educational decision making. In A. Thomas & J. Grimes (Eds.), *Best practices in school psychology* (4th ed., pp. 377–387). Bethesda, MD: National Association of School Psychologists.

Huebner, E. S. (1992). Leadership skills for school psychologists: Improving parental involvement in multi-disciplinary team interactions. In S. Christenson & J. Close Conoley (Eds.), *Home-school collaboration: Enhancing children's academic and social competence* (pp. 409–422) Bethesda, MD: National Association of School Psychologists.

Jenson, B. F., & Potter, M. L. (1990). Best practices in communicating with parents. In A. Thomas & J. Grimes (Eds.), *Best practices in school psychology* (2nd ed., pp. 183–193). Bethesda, MD: National Association of School Psychologists.

Lake, J. F. (2000). An analysis of factors that contribute to parent-school conflict in special education. *Remedial and Special Education, 20*(4), 240–252.

Lakoff, R. T. (1990). *Talking power: The politics of language in our lives.* New York: Harper Collins.

Lovitt, T. C. (1999). Parents of youth with disabilities: Their perceptions of school programs. *Remedial and Special Education, 20*(3), 134–143.

Margolis, H. (1998). Avoiding special education due process hearings: Lessons from the field. *Journal of Educational and Psychological Consultation, 9*(3), 233–260.

Merker, B. M., Hanson, W. E., & Poston, J. M. (2010). National survey of psychologists' training and practice in breaking bad news: A mixed methods study of the MUM effect. *Journal of Clinical Psychology in Medical Settings,* 17, 211–219.

Miller, D. D., & Kraft, N. P. (2014). Best practices in partnering with parents in school-based services. In P. Harrison & A. Thomas (Eds.), *Best practices in school psychology: Systems-level services* (pp. 479–489). Bethesda, MD: National Association of School Psychologists.

Minke, K. M. (2000). Preventing school problems and promoting school success through family-school-community collaboration. In K. Minke & G. Bear (Eds.) *Preventing school problems-promoting school success* (pp. 377–420). Bethesda, MD: National Association of School Psychologists.

Minke, K. M. & Jenson, K. L. (2014). Best practices in facilitating family-school meetings. In P. Harrison & A. Thomas (Eds.), *Best practices in school psychology: Systems-level services* (pp. 505–518). Bethesda, MD: National Association of School Psychologists.

Nowell, B. L. & Salem, D. A. (2007). The impact of special education mediation on parent-school relationships-Parents' Perspective. *Remedial and Special Education, 28*(5), 304–315.

Phillips, E. (2008). When parents aren't enough: External advocacy in special education. *Yale Law Journal, 117*(8), 1802–1853.

Pollak, J. M. (1988). The feedback process with parents in child and adolescent psychological assessment. *Psychology in the Schools, 25,* 143–153.

Pruitt, P., Wandry, D., & Hollums, D. (1998). Listen to us! Parents speak out about their interactions with special educators. *Preventing School Failure, 42*(4), 161–167.

Rappaport, J. (1981). In praise of paradox: A social policy of empowerment over prevention. *American Journal of Community Psychology, 9*(1), 1–25.

Salisbury, D. F., & Branson, R. K. (1997). Applying customer dissatisfaction measures to schools: You better know what's wrong before you try to fix it. *Educational Policy, 11*(3), 286–309.

Sands, R. G. (1988). Sociolinguistic analysis of a mental health interview. *Social Work, 33,* 149–154.

Sands, R. G. (1994). A comparison of interprofessional and team-parent talk of an interdisciplinary team. *Social Work in Education, 16*(4), 207–220.

Seligman, M., & Darling, R. B. (1997). *Ordinary families, special children.* New York: Guilford Press.

Shaver, E. A. (2015). Every day counts: Proposals to reform IDEA's due process structure. *Case Western Reserve Law Review, 66*(1), 143–208.

Sheridan, S. M., Clarke, B. L., & Christenson, S. L. (2014). Best practices in promoting family engagement in education. In P. Harrison & A. Thomas (Eds.), *Best practices in school psychology: Systems-level services* (pp. 439–453). Bethesda, MD: National Association of School Psychologists.

Silverstein, J., Springer, J., & Russo, N. (1992). Involving parents in the special education process. In S. Christenson & J. Close Conoley (Eds.), *Home-school collaboration: Enhancing children's academic and social competence* (pp. 383–408) Bethesda, MD: National Association of School Psychologists.

Spann, S., Kohler, F. W., & Soenksen, D. (2003). Examining parents' involvement in and perceptions of special education services: An interview with families in a parent support group. *Focus on Autism and Other Developmental Disabilities, 18*(4), 228–237.

Stallard, P. (2001). Reducing parental dissatisfaction with a child and adolescent psychology service: A process of quality improvement. *Journal of Mental Health, 10*(1), 63–74.

Stanovich, P. J. (1996). Collaboration-the key to successful instruction in today's inclusive schools. *Intervention in School and Clinic, 32*(1), 39–43.

Steiber, S. R., & Krowinski, W. J. (1990). *Measuring and managing patient satisfaction.* American Hospital Publishing.

Swap, S. M. (1992). Parent involvement and success for all children: What we all know. In S. Christenson & J. Close Conoley (Eds.), *Home-school collaboration: Enhancing children's academic and social competence* (pp. 53–82). Bethesda, MD: National Association of School Psychologists.

Tharinger, D. J., Finn, S. E., Hersh, B., Wilkinson, A., Christopher, G. B., & Tran, A. (2008). Assessment feedback with parents and preadolescent children: A collaborative approach. *Professional Psychology: Research and Practice, 39*(6), 600–609.

Turnbull, A. P., & Turnbull, H. R. (1986). *Families, professionals, and exceptionality a special partnership.* Columbus, OH: Merrill Publishing.

Valle, J. W. (2011). Down the rabbit hole: A commentary about research on parents and special education. *Learning Disability Quarterly, 34*(3), 183–190.

Vickers, H. S., Minke, K. M., & Anderson, K. J. (2002). Best practices in facilitating collaborative family-teacher routine conferences. In A. Thomas & J. Grimes (Eds.), *Best practices in school psychology* (4th ed., pp. 431–449). Bethesda, MD: Author.

Weill, M. (1999). Parent-teacher meetings: Dos and don'ts. In A. S. Cantor & S. A. Carroll (Eds.), *Helping children at home and school: Handouts from your school psychologist* (p. 79). Bethesda, MD: National Association of School Psychologists.

Westling, D. L. (1997). What parents of young children with mental disabilities want: The views of one community. *Focus on Autism and Other Developmental Disabilities, 12*(2), 67–80.

Ysseldyke, J., Algozzine, B., & Mitchell, J. (1982). Special education team decision making: An analysis of current practice. *Personnel and Guidance Journal, 60*, 308–313.

5 Prerequisite Practitioner Skills to Utilizing the Feedback Model

The current chapter builds upon previously reviewed concepts while introducing skills and practices that are prerequisite to successful implementation of the Feedback Model. These skills and practices are categorized in terms of "content" and "process." Content skills refer to the practitioner's factual knowledge base of assessment in general, the factor structure of the instruments, constructs measured by each instrument, and classification ranges for standardized scores. The development of content skills will require the practitioner to intentionally learn concepts and become fluent with explaining them in an easily understandable manner. Alternatively, process skills consist of basic counseling techniques such as listening, paraphrasing, summarizing, and reframing. Process skills are developed through supervised training and their utilization during feedback will be dependent on practitioners' ability to self-regulate their emotions. This chapter reviews specific content and process related skills and emphasizes the use of easily understandable language. Specific verbiage for explaining complex constructs is also included along with a section describing language etiquette.

Content Related Skills

Successful implementation of the Feedback Model requires the practitioner to be fluent in explaining basic principles of the normal curve and characteristics of standardized scores, percentile ranks, and confidence intervals. Furthermore, basic competencies in explaining the descriptive categories of standard scores, common constructs measured during the evaluation, and factor structures to popular assessment instruments are a necessity. A discussion of each of these topics follows and recommendations for specific verbiage are offered. Note that each topic is briefly reviewed and the reader is referred to well-established resources for greater details (Reynolds & Livingston, 2014; Sattler, 2018).

Principles of the Normal Curve

Utilizing the Feedback Model during a feedback session with parents will require practitioners to have working-knowledge of the normal curve, as the results from the psycho-educational evaluation will largely be obtained from standardized instruments. In its simplest sense, the normal-curve is a symmetrical frequency distribution of scores that can be applied to a variety of human characteristics and traits. An equal number of scores fall above and below the midpoint of the curve which represents the mean, median, and mode of the score distribution. Specific percentages of scores on each side of the mean are then divided into standard deviations. With these parameters, the following characteristics of the normal curve are noted and should be committed to memory.

- 50% of the scores fall above the mean and 50% of scores fall below the mean.
- Of the 50% of scores below the mean, approximately 34% of scores fall between the mean and -1 standard deviation, 14% of the scores fall between -1 and -2 standard deviations, and 2% of scores fall between -2 and -3 standard deviations.
- Of the 50% of scores above the mean, approximately 34% of scores fall between the mean and 1 standard deviation, 14% of the scores fall between 1 and 2 standard deviations, and 2% of scores fall between 2 and 3 standard deviations.
- 68% of scores fall between $\pm$ 1 standard deviation from the mean.
- 96% of scores fall between $\pm$ 2 standard deviations from the mean.
- 99% of the scores fall between $\pm$ 3 standard deviations from the mean.
- The normal curve theoretically extends beyond $\pm$ 3 standard deviations from the mean; however, these scores are rare.

When applying these principles of the normal curve to an every-day setting, practitioners can make general assumptions about the population's characteristics. Consider the following examples using a school district that enrolls 1000 students. Given that a diagnostic criterion for Intellectual Disability is an overall level of intellectual functioning of 70 or below, then one would estimate approximately 20 of those students to be identified as meeting the criteria for Intellectual Disability, as an overall level of intellectual functioning of 70 is typically two standard deviations below the mean and representative of 2 percent of the population. Alternatively, using the same school district, one would estimate approximately 20 students to meet the criteria for Intellectually Gifted, as a diagnostic criterion for Intellectually Gifted often is an overall level of intellectual functioning of 130 or greater which is typically two standard deviations above the mean and representative of 2 percent of the population. In both instances, principles of the normal curve provide basic reference points to help understand the expected prevalence characteristics within a given population.

In a similar manner, principles of the normal curve help to shape the feedback process with parents when utilizing the Feedback Model. Note that with the Feedback Model, practitioners create a horizontal graph with descriptive ranges while in the presence of the parent, rather than referring to visual depiction of the normal curve. While creating this horizontal graph and describing the descriptive ranges in Step 7 of the Feedback Model, practitioners might state to parents,

If we were to evaluate all of the students in the school, 96% of the students' performance would fall across the Very Low, Low Average, Average, High

Average, and Very High Ranges … and when scores fall outside of these ranges [referring to the Extremely Low and Extremely High Ranges], we consider performance to be significantly different than what would be expected from a child his or her age.

Characteristics of Standardized Scores and Percentile Ranks

Implementing the Feedback Model requires practitioners to be well versed in standard scores and percentile ranks. Standard scores are rooted in the principles of the normal curve and have a fixed mean and standard deviation. Most popular measures of intelligence and achievement, such as the Wechsler, Woodcock-Johnson, and Kaufman scales yield broad composite standard scores that have a mean of 100 and a standard deviation of 15. This is also true for common measures of visual-motor and adaptive functioning, such as the Beery-Buktenica Developmental Test of Visual-Motor Integration-Sixth Edition, the Vineland Adaptive Behavior Scales-Third Edition and the Adaptive Behavior Assessment System-Third Edition. Alternatively, narrow and broadband social-emotional rating scales, such as the Conners-Third Edition and the Behavior Assessment System for Children-Third Edition, yield composite and subscale scores according to the T-scale with a mean of 50 and a standard deviation of 10.

With knowledge of the normal curve and the mean and standard deviation of any scale of measurement, practitioners have the capacity to translate and compare scores of different instruments. For example, a standard score of 115 on an adaptive behavior measure is equivalent to a standard score of 60 on a social-emotional rating scale, as both scores are one standard deviation above the mean. Similarly, a standard score of 70 on an adaptive behavior measure ($M = 100$; $SD = 15$) is equivalent to a standard score of 30 on a social-emotional rating scale ($M = 50$; $SD = 10$). Through having a firm understanding of the relationship among standard scores of different scales, practitioners are better able to utilize the Feedback Model which explains scores to parents through using descriptive ranges (i.e. Average Range, Low Average Range, etc).

The Feedback Model does not utilize percentile ranks as the primary medium when explaining evaluation results to parents; although, practitioners may use percentile ranks to further explain individual standard scores after they are plotted. A percentile rank represents a "point in a distribution at or below which the scores of a given percentage of individuals fall" (Sattler, 2018, p. 105). As such, if a student's Broad Written Language skills tested to be within the Average Range (standard score = 107) and at a percentile rank of 69, then his or her overall written language skills were measured at a level that *equals or exceeds* 69 percent of others in the standardization sample. In this example, it is imperative that practitioners use the words *equals or exceeds* when describing percentile ranks, as the percentile rank indicates that the student performed as well as or better than 69 percent of similar aged others in the standardization sample.

Percentile ranks can sometimes be misleading in comparison to standard scores when explaining evaluation results to parents. Unlike standard scores, the units in a percentile rank distribution are not equal and consistent with a normal distribution. Consider the following example utilizing standard scores with a mean of 100 and a standard deviation of 15. In this instance given principles of the normal curve, it would be expected that the score of 85 would be equivalent to a percentile rank of 16. However, on the Calculation subtest of the Woodcock-Johnson IV Test of Achievement, a standard score of 86 is equivalent to a percentile rank of 18. This characteristic is common among all standardized instruments including social-emotional behavior scales; thus, promoting the use of standard scores as the primary means to explain evaluation results to parents.

If practitioners choose to use percentile ranks as a supplemental means to explain evaluation results to parents during a feedback session, then it is recommended that they disclose to the parent the nuances of percentile ranks versus standard scores. Furthermore, practitioners are reminded to describe the percentile rank in terms of performance that *equals or exceeds* a specific point. An effective manner to share this information is as follows.

> Ralph's math calculation skills tested within the Low Average Range [standard score 86] and at a level that equaled or exceeded 18% of others in the standardization sample. This means that when standing in a line of 100 other similar aged students who completed the Calculation subtest, 72 others would be in front of him.

Confidence Intervals

As will be described in Chapter 6, the Feedback Model does not require practitioners to explicitly state the standardized scores that were obtained from the comprehensive psycho-educational evaluation. Parents are provided tables of scores in the psycho-educational evaluation report which they can read at their own leisure. Emphasizing specific scores during the feedback process is believed to overload most parents' short-term working memory capacity, as it would be unfair to expect them to have an operational understanding of the normal curve and standardized scores beforehand. However, in some cases, parents will demand that the practitioner share a specific score during the feedback session, particularly on a measure of cognitive functioning. In such cases, the practitioner is first recommended to remind parents that the scores are in the detailed psycho-educational report and the purpose of the feedback session is to provide parents "with the tools to better understand the psycho-educational report at a later time." Afterwards, the practitioner should immediately comply with the parents' request to avoid any distrust on the parents' behalf.

Whenever practitioners share specific scores with parents during the feedback session, they are obligated to describe the confidence interval around the obtained score, as the score is not perfectly accurate due to inherent measurement error (Sattler, 2018). Practitioners can typically choose to select confidence intervals at the 68 percent, 90 percent, or 95 percent level depending on the degree of certainty desired. As suspected, a 95 percent confidence interval has the highest likelihood of including the child's "true" performance and it is recommended in the majority of cases. Thus, a 95 percent confidence interval is conceptualized as the range in which a child's "true" score will exist 95 percent of the time. Keeping with the same example of Ralph which was used earlier, practitioners would state the following when explaining confidence intervals to parents as part of the Feedback Model.

> Each time we report specific scores, we also need to describe the confidence interval around them. In Ralph's case the 95% confidence interval was chosen. Ralph's performance on the Calculation subtest was in the Low Average Range with an earned standard score of 86. If Ralph was administered the Calculation subtest 100 times, 95 times out of 100, Ralph would earn a score between 78 and 94. Five times out of 100, his score would be outside of this range.

Descriptive Categories of Standardized Scores

Practitioners will utilize multiple norm referenced instruments when conducting a comprehensive psycho-educational evaluation within and across evaluation domains (i.e. cognitive, academic, visual-motor, social emotional, and behavioral). Each of these instruments has a unique descriptive classification system to describe the subsequent scores. Thus, similar scores on different instruments measuring the same construct may be assigned different descriptive categories. For example, the Wechsler Individual Scale of Intelligence-Fifth Edition (WISC-V) has the following descriptive classification system for scores (Wechsler, 2014).

- 130 and above = Extremely High
- 120–129 = Very High
- 110–119 = High Average
- 90–109 = Average
- 80–89 = Low Average
- 70–79 = Very Low
- 69 and below = Extremely Low

Alternatively, the Woodcock-Johnson Test of Cognitive Abilities-Fourth Edition (WJ-IV) uses the following descriptive classification system for scores (Mather & Wendling, 2014).

- 131 and above = Very Superior
- 121–130 = Superior
- 111–120 = High Average
- 90–110 = Average
- 80–89 = Low Average
- 70–79 = Low
- 69 and below = Very Low

When reviewing the descriptive classification system for the WISC-V and WJ-IV, it is evident that the names of the descriptive classification ranges for scores vary as the scores move further from the mean. This characteristic is true for most instruments and this variance could cause the parent confusion during a feedback session if both instruments were used during the comprehensive psycho-educational evaluation, as scores in the 70s on the WISC are described as Very Low Range and scores in the 70s on the WJ-IV are labelled in the Low Range. To alleviate this issue, it is recommended that when practitioners utilize the Feedback Model, they utilize only one descriptive classification system to describe the results from all of the instruments utilized in the comprehensive psycho-educational evaluation. It is most sensible for that descriptive classification system to be the one associated with the primary cognitive measure administered during the evaluation because of the inherent relationship among cognitive ability, academic skills, and social-emotional and behavioral functioning. In sum, if practitioners administered the full WISC-V, supplemental subtests of the WJ-IV, the Wechsler Individual Achievement Test-Third Edition (WIAT-III), the Developmental Test of Visual Motor Integration, and the BASC-III during a comprehensive psycho-educational evaluation, then explanation of the results through the Feedback Model should occur via the descriptive classification categories associated with the WISC-V.

In Step 7 of the Feedback Model, practitioners draw a graph in the presence of the parent, label the left margins with the descriptive classification ranges, and explain what performance in each range entails. Thus, it is critical that the practitioner have the numerical ranges associated with each descriptive classification category committed to memory along with a brief parent-friendly explanation of the descriptive classification categories themselves. Sample verbiage for the WJ-IV Tests of Cognitive Abilities is offered below and practitioners can easily adapt this verbiage to be used with other cognitive measures that may be utilized in a comprehensive psycho-educational evaluation.

- *131 and above = Very Superior Range.* Performance in the Very Superior Range suggests skills that are significantly above what would be expected given your child's age.
- *121–130 = Superior Range.* Performance in the Superior Range suggests skills and abilities that are developed at a level above what would be expected given your child's age.
- *111–120 = High Average Range.* Scores falling in the High Average Range suggest skills and abilities that are age-appropriate, except the child may complete tasks faster or more efficiently, be successful with abstract tasks, require less-direct instruction and practice, and generalize information more readily without prompting.
- *90–110 = Average Range.* Performance in the Average Range indicates that the child is performing at a level consistent with his or her age. The child is right where he or she should be.
- *80–89 = Low Average Range.* Scores falling in the Low Average Range suggest skills and abilities that are age appropriate, except the child may complete tasks slower and less efficiently, be more successful with concrete rather than abstract concepts, require more direct instruction and practice, and have difficulty generalizing information without prompting.
- *70–79 = Low Range.* When skills and abilities test in the Low Range, this is when we start to demonstrate concern, as performance is below what would be expected given your child's age.

- *69 and below = Very Low Range.* Performance in the Very Low Range suggests significantly underdeveloped skills and abilities when compared to what would be expected given your child's age.

Common Constructs Measured During the Evaluation

At minimum, comprehensive psycho-educational evaluations measure skills in the cognitive, academic, visual-motor, and social-emotional domains. Additional domains, such as auditory and visual processing, phonological awareness, memory, and executive functioning, may also be examined depending on the complexity of the evaluation's referral questions. Thus, the practitioner's repertoire of skills must include the ability to explain to parents the constructs measured in a clear and understandable manner. This task is often challenging for beginning practitioners as they seem to struggle with finding simple language and real-life examples to sufficiently depict the construct without losing its essence. Practitioners utilizing the Feedback Model will need to explain the constructs measured during the evaluation when completing Steps 9 through 15. Thus, parent-friendly verbiage for explaining common constructs measured during an evaluation is offered below and practitioners are encouraged to carefully note the language and adapt the explanations to their individual cases as they see fit. Note that the language offered is considered only to be a starting point and additional details along with abstract concepts should be included with parents who already possess a basic understanding of the content reviewed. The following discussion will begin with addressing the ten broad cognitive abilities and then proceed to the academic, visual-motor, and social-emotional domains. Practitioners will need to adapt the following content to match the specific instruments utilized in the psycho-educational evaluation, as composite scores of instruments differ in their specific subtest arrangement.

Intelligence / Cognitive Functioning

- *Overall level of intellectual or cognitive functioning.* As part of the evaluation, we measured how smart [student name] is, or his or her intellectual or cognitive functioning. Intelligence or cognitive functioning is central to our ability to adapt to demands in different environments and it is inherently connected to our receptiveness towards academic instruction.
- *Crystalized Knowledge (Gc).* Crystalized Knowledge exists within one's overall level of intelligence or cognitive functioning. Crystalized Knowledge is basic-ally the amount of information that one has acquired through language in his or her academic and home environments. Folks with well-developed Crystalized Knowledge usually are successful with fact-based tasks.
- *Fluid Reasoning Ability (Gf).* Fluid Reasoning Ability exists within one's overall level of intelligence or cognitive functioning. Fluid Reasoning Ability typic-ally involves problem-solving and the ability to "think on your feet." Folks with well-developed Fluid Reasoning Ability are often successful applying previously learned information to new situations.

- *Short-Term Memory (Gsm).* Short-Term Memory skills are part of one's overall level of intelligence or cognitive functioning. Short-Term Memory examines the amount of information that we can store and effectively retrieve within a short duration of time. Students with strong short-term memory skills are usually attentive and capable of holding information in immediate memory to then be used within a few seconds.
- *Long-Term Storage and Retrieval (Glr).* Long-Term Storage and Retrieval skills are often included in one's overall level of intelligence or cognitive functioning. Long-Term Storage and Retrieval provides us with insight regarding one's ability to store and then fluently retrieve new or previously learned information. Success in this domain is typically an indicator of one's general learning potential.
- *Visual Processing (Gv).* Many instruments include Visual Processing as part of one's overall level of intelligence or cognitive functioning. Visual Processing is one's capacity to work with simple and complex visual problems that commonly involve memory, rotation, and estimation. Visual Processing skills commonly help us to complete puzzles.
- *Auditory Processing (Ga).* Tasks specifically measuring Auditory Processing skills are often supplementary to popular instruments examining overall intelligence or cognitive functioning. Auditory Processing is prerequisite to well-developed reading skills and it involves speech sound discrimination and memory for sound patterns.
- *Processing Speed (Gs).* Processing Speed is the part of one's overall level of intelligence or cognitive functioning that allows us to complete boring, timed tasks quickly and efficiently. Success with these types of tasks requires attention, concentration, and motivation.
- *Quantitative Knowledge (Gq).* Quantitative Knowledge is often supplementary to popular instruments examining overall intelligence or cognitive functioning. Quantitative knowledge is the ability to utilize already acquired mathematical knowledge specifically through estimation, number facility, and reasoning.
- *Reading and Writing (Grw).* Specific measures of reading and writing are supplementary to popular measures of intelligence or cognitive functioning. This domain examines one's ability to read and write.
- *Decision Speed/Reaction Time (Gt).* Specific measures of Decision Speed and Reaction Time are supplementary to popular measures of intelligence or cognitive functioning. This domain examines the ability to quickly react to stimuli in seconds or fractions of a second.

Academic Functioning

- *Overall Level of Academic Functioning.* Most popular measures of academic functioning yield a broad achievement score which represents students' average performance across all academic skills measured. Think of this score as if your child earned one grade for his or her performance across all subjects during a particular quarter, semester, or trimester. Although this score helps us understand students' general level of academic functioning, it is not as specific as domain scores in reading, mathematics, written language, and oral language.

- *Reading Composite.* Popular measures of achievement yield an overall or broad reading score that represents performance across word identification, reading comprehension, and reading fluency subtests. These subtests typically require the student to read word lists of increasing difficulty, answer questions after reading a passage or supply a missing word that makes sense to complete the passage, and accurately read sentences or passages within given time-limits.
- *Mathematics Composite.* The mathematics composite score represents performance across mathematics' calculation, application, and fluency subtests. These subtests commonly require students to solve math problems of increasing difficulty using paper and pencil, respond to word problems by applying mathematical concepts and operations, and complete basic math calculation tasks within a given time-limit.
- *Written Language Composite.* The Written Language Composite score represents performance across spelling, written expression, and writing fluency subtests. These subtests typically require students to spell words of increasing difficulty dictated by the examiner, compose sentences or paragraphs after provided prompts, and write meaningful sentences or paragraphs within a given time-limit.
- *Oral Language Composite.* The Oral Language Composite score typically represents performance across listening comprehension and oral expression subtests. These subtests often require students to listen to and repeat sentences or short passages, use words to identify pictures of objects, and explain activities after provided prompts. It may also be necessary for students to generate word lists with a common theme during a given-time limit.

Visual-Motor Skills

- *Overall Visual-Motor Functioning.* Comprehensive psycho-educational evaluations commonly include a measure of Visual-Motor Functioning to help identify if visual-motor skills are adversely affecting students' performance within the curriculum. To do so, students are usually required to draw increasing complex geometric figures without erasing. Performance on visual-motor tasks lets us know if students can accurately recreate information presented to them visually.

Social-Emotional Functioning

- *Social-Emotional Functioning.* A students' Social-Emotional Functioning is evaluated through observations while working with the examiner, observations in the home and school setting, and interviews and rating scales of the parent, teacher, completed by the student, parent, and teacher. From the data collected, we are basically looking to see if the student's behavior is significantly different than what would be expected given his or her age. Thus, we explore how the student gets along with peers and adults, if there is anything that is preventing academic success other than intellectual, health, or sensory factors, and if there are unusual behaviors under normal circumstances. We also look to see if there are noteworthy fears related to the academic environment and if an unusual amount of sadness or depression is evident.

Process Related Skills

In addition to having proficiency with content related knowledge, successful implementation of the Feedback Model requires practitioners to possess basic competencies with related process skills. Process skills, sometimes referred to as clinical skills, are first developed through didactive learning and then further honed through experience and supervised training. The importance of process skills within practitioners' repertoires cannot be overstated, as these skills are necessary for practitioners to navigate their emotional interface with parents during the feedback meeting.

Practitioners must be aware of the emotional reactions that parents have towards them and their own emotional reactions towards the parent. These emotional reactions may serve as underlying threads that transverse home-school relationships and special education team meetings. Emotional reactions between service provider and service recipient have been widely recognized in various schools of family therapy and doctor-patient relationships (Freud, 1966; Goleman, 1995; Jung, 1933; Nichols & Davis, 2016). Quite often, these emotional reactions are distorted and may stem from unresolved early family relations and/or conflicts of the unconscious on behalf of the service provider and service recipient (Freud, 1966; Jung, 1933; Nichols & Davis, 2016). As applied to feedback meetings, parents of children with needs might cast anger, blame, and resentment onto other team members during discussion of evaluation results and recommendations. The team members might then respond to these reactions by becoming defensive and critical of the parents, thereby creating a hostile home-school relationship and limiting the likelihood of parent satisfaction with psycho-educational evaluation process.

To maintain positive parent perceptions of the professional and avoid adverse home-school relationships and eventually parent dissatisfaction, practitioners must prepare themselves for their emotional interaction with parents. Practitioners must be cognizant of their beliefs, values, and personality traits and they must be mindful of how these characteristics interface with parents' emotional functioning. They need to recognize how each of these components manifest in daily interactions and have the potential of influencing the behavior and perceptions of others, especially parents. Thus, practitioners must have a personal intra-psychic awareness and be familiar with how they react to qualities and traits of others. Ultimately, practitioners should strive to be emotionally involved "in" the family, but not "of" the family (Nichols & Davis, 2016). To accomplish this task, practitioners need to ultimately identify with the parents of children referred for evaluation. Identification with parents begins through empathy on behalf of themselves. Practitioners empathize when they realize that parents are doing their best given their circumstances and they ask themselves, "What would I like or need if I was that parent?" (Dunst, Trivette, & LaPointe, 1994; Nichols & Davis, 2016).

Additional strategies are offered to further induce positive parent perceptions of the practitioner and avoid an adverse emotional interface between parent and practitioner, given recommendations from other researchers (Fish, 1995; Glazer, 2014; Huebner, 1992; Kroth, 1985; Nichols & Davis, 2016; Pollack, 1988; Sachs-Wise, 1995; Tharinger, Finn, Hersh, Wilkinson, Christopher, & Tran, 2008).

Practitioners are encouraged to establish communication with parents as early as possible. Early communication will enhance the relationship building process and give practitioners the opportunity to recognize and remediate any adverse feelings they may have towards the parents before the time of the meeting. If negative feelings exist, then it may be worthwhile to tactfully express these feelings to the parents. Hidden feelings might be unintentionally acted-out during meetings and result in adverse emotional responses from parents. Expressed feelings have a likelihood of remaining benign (Nichols & Davis, 2016). However, often times, negative emotional reactions to parents are not easily recognized in order to be expressed. Therefore, it may be necessary for practitioners to collaborate with colleagues and supervisors to anticipate and/or negotiate hidden emotional negativity (Nichols & Davis, 2016). Collaboration helps modulate the emotional distance between team members and parents to facilitate objectivity of the service providers.

Outside of improving their self-awareness and seeking collaboration to manage the emotional interaction with the parent, practitioners are encouraged to continuously develop their basic counseling skills, such as listening, paraphrasing, reframing, and summarizing. Each of these skills will need to be overlearned, as their utilization during the feedback process will be dependent on practitioners' ability to self-regulate their own emotions.

Listening

Kroth (1985) has described four different stages to listening and emphasized that individuals vacillate among the stages during a conversation, rather than remain fixated at a particular stage. The four stages have been categorized as: 1) passive listening, 2) active listening, 3) passive non-listening, and 4) active non-listening (Kroth, 1985).

Active and passive listening have commonalities and differences. In both, the listener appears attentive to the conversation, typically leans forward towards the speaker, and offers nonverbal signs of acceptance (Kroth, 1985; Vickers, Minke, & Anderson, 2002). Active and passive listening differ in terms of the listener's engagement in the conversation, as active listening involves the reflection of feelings and the listener's involvement in identifying and clarifying the speaker's problems (Kroth, 1985; Vickers, Minke, & Anderson, 2002).

Characteristics of active and passive non-listening are more distinct. With passive non-listening, the listener seems to hear what is being said, but he/she may demonstrate limited signs of nonverbal acceptance while being inattentive to the "feeling" within the message of the speaker (Kroth, 1985; Vickers, Minke, & Anderson, 2002). In contrast, active non-listening might be described best in terms of the "cocktail party" effect (Kroth, 1985). Conversation is typically superficial in nature when the "cocktail party" effect occurs. People appear to be polite and talk "to" each other, but they do not talk "with" each other (Kroth, 1985). As suggested by parents' comments within the literature and personal experience, professionals at special education team meetings seem to best fit the criteria for passive listening and passive non-listening. Although practitioners appear to be listening to parent concerns, they typically do not become actively involved in problem clarification and identification. Thus, meetings are often inefficient and unproductive in terms of problem solving. Additionally, professionals seem insensitive to the underlying feelings conveyed in the parents' messages, as professionals have been noted to lack empathy and understanding towards family needs (Cameron & Orr, 1991; Darling, 1988; Phillips, 2008; Pruitt, Wandry, & Hollums, 1998; Seligman & Darling, 1997). It is very possible that passive listening and passive non-listening are characteristic of meetings that involve more than two individuals and focus on discussing sensitive topics of a personal nature.

Practitioners must strive to be active listeners while delivering feedback of psycho-educational evaluation results to the parent, as it is essential for the parent to feel that he or she has been heard. To do so, practitioners can utilize nonverbal and verbal techniques to convey their attentiveness to the parent's communication. Nonverbal techniques include maintaining appropriate eye contact, leaning inward toward the parent, head nodding, and smiling. Alternatively, with verbal techniques, the practitioner might use statements that encourage the parent to continue speaking, such as "Tell me more," "Please explain," "How so," and "I see." While applying these techniques, the practitioner is then encouraged to paraphrase, reframe, and summarize the content of the parent's communication.

Paraphrasing

Often during the feedback session, the parent might share extraneous information during conversation and it will be necessary for the practitioner to utilize the paraphrasing technique. Paraphrasing occurs when the practitioner restates the "jist" of what the parent has said (Teyber & Teyber, 2017). As such, paraphrasing communicates to the parent that the practitioner is listening, allows the practitioner to clarify confusing content shared by the parent, emphasizes issues through the practitioner restating them more concisely, and serves as a method for the practitioner to check on his or her accuracy of the information heard. The paraphrase should not be too lengthy, as it will lead the parent to stop speaking and discontinue the flow of conversation. Alternatively, the paraphrase should not be too short because it will inadequately represent the content of the conversation and lead to parent confusion. Consider the following example.

PARENT: I just don't know about her teacher. Sometimes she seems very friendly and interested in supporting Caroline's needs and the next time she ignores me like I don't exist.

PRACTITIONER (*appropriate paraphrase*): You haven't experienced her as being very consistent.

PRACTITIONER (*inappropriate paraphrase*): Teaching is an extremely stressful job and I know Caroline's teacher, she has been here for over 25 years and worked with thousands of students, I am sure that she did not mean to be curt with you.

In the above example, the appropriate paraphrase succinctly restates the parent's concern, validates the parent, and introduces the practitioner's interpretation of the parent's impression of the teacher as inconsistent. In comparison, the inappropriate paraphrase is too lengthy and attempts to defend the teacher's behavior; thus, introducing an additional topic of potential conflict (i.e. stressors of teaching) that the parent may choose to address; thereby, potentially derailing the original conversation.

Reframing

It is not uncommon during the feedback process for the parent to be overly pessimistic in his or her description of the child's characteristics, the school, the practitioner, or the evaluation results. In such cases, practitioners will need to reframe the parent's content of conversation. Reframing is a cognitive technique used to help create an alternative means of perceiving a situation, as an individual's point of view is dependent on the *frame* through which experiences are viewed (Teyber & Teyber, 2017). When the *frame* is shifted, meaning is altered and changes in thinking and behavior theoretically follow. The following example illustrates a practitioner appropriately reframing a parent's perception of the school during a feedback meeting.

PARENT: I just wish that the school would do its job and help my child. Instead, they are constantly nagging me to complete all of these forms and attend these meetings.

PRACTITIONER: Isn't it comforting to have a school that is focused on your child's success and values your input as a parent

Summarizing

Practitioners will inevitably need to utilize summarization skills during the feedback session, as they may be presented with new information from the parent about the child's history and educational experiences. Summarization combines two or more of the parent's thoughts, feelings or behaviors into a general theme— integrating the content of the information shared by the parent and helping the practitioner validate his or her perception of the information shared by the parent (Teyber & Teyber, 2017). Summarization will also be used to close the feedback session upon presenting the parent with the conclusions and recommendations of the evaluation. Consider the following example.

PARENT: We have been through this process so many times … and everyone tells us something different. One evaluation said that my daughter has autism and another said that she is dyslexic. She hates school and I don't blame her.

PRACTITIONER: Your daughter has been through multiple evaluations in the past and the results have suggested different conclusions. The current evaluation has considered the previous results in addition to collecting new data; thus, leading the new conclusions to be more substantial—hopefully providing you with some closure in specifically identifying your child's strengths and needs.

Language Etiquette

As discussed throughout the previous chapters, the language used to communicate the evaluation results to parents must be clear and easily understandable in order to avoid confusion on the parent's behalf. Taken further, the practitioner's language choices should intentionally avoid words and phrases that have potential negative connotations or trigger adverse emotional reactions by the parent. Table 5.1 provides a list of common terms and suggested alternatives for practitioners to utilize during the feedback process. Note that this list is not exhaustive and the practitioner will likely generate additional entries and alternatives as further experience is obtained in delivering psycho-educational evaluation results to parents.

In addition to these common terms and recommended alternatives, practitioners are encouraged to avoid using the first person (i.e. I, me) when explaining the evaluation results to parents. Doing so, sends parents the message that the practitioner is solely responsible for the conclusions and recommendations of the evaluation; thus, making the focus of the evaluation about the practitioner, rather than the child and subsequent data. When the parent perceives the practitioner to be solely responsible for the evaluation results, the practitioner then becomes the lone target of parent frustration and conflict when the evaluation's conclusions and recommendations are inconsistent with parents' original expectations.

Table 5.1 Common Terms and Suggested Alternatives

Common Terms	Suggested Alternatives
Always	Frequently, majority of the time
Criminal charges	Legal infractions
Expulsion (school)	Discipline infraction
Failure	Lack of success
Home-maker	Stay-at-home mom/dad
Husband/wife	Partner
Immature	Seemed younger than his/her chronological age
Intelligence/Cognitive Functioning	How smart the child is
Lazy	Limited effort
Low	Below expectations
Messy	Unkept, unorganized
Never	Infrequently, hardly-ever
Poor	Underdeveloped, limited, challenged, struggled
Poverty	Limited resources
Subtest	Task
Suspension (school)	Discipline infraction
Test (noun)	Instrument
Testing (noun)	Assessment, Evaluation
Unemployed	Not-working
Unmotivated	Put forth limited effort
Weakness	Challenge, limitation, struggle
Well-rounded	Involved, regularly participates

Practitioners should also avoid describing the evaluation results in terms of opinion. In other words, practitioners should not state, "In the opinion of this examiner, [student] meets eligibility criteria for [specific disability category as per IDEA regulations]." The conclusions and recommendations of the evaluation are based on standardized procedures, data-based decision making, and evidence-based interventions—all of which are critically reviewed in the discipline specific literature of our field. Data-based decisions are qualitatively different than mere opinions and such decisions should not be diluted by explaining them as simple opinion.

Summary

Chapter 5 reviewed content knowledge and process skills deemed necessary for successful implementation of the Feedback Model. Principles of the normal curve and characteristics of standard scores and percentile ranks were discussed along with the operational definitions of the descriptive categories for standardized score results. Parent-friendly verbiage for explaining common constructs measured during a comprehensive psycho-educational evaluation was highlighted and basic counseling skills such as listening, paraphrasing, reframing, and summarizing were presented with supplemental real-life examples. The chapter concluded with a review of language etiquette and offered suggested alternatives for common words and phrases that may elicit negative emotional reactions on behalf of the parent.

At this point in time, the reader should recognize that delivering feedback results to parents following a comprehensive psycho-educational evaluation is a complex and dynamic process that requires preparation, competency in describing scores and their related attributes, an ability to fluently describe the constructs measured, and sensitivity towards parents' emotional needs. These skills in-and-of-themselves are insufficient to be successful with the feedback process, as the feedback session also requires an imposed structure to make the content of the feedback presentation meaningful to the parent. The Feedback Model will provide this needed structure and an in-depth review of its implementation will be provided in the next chapter.

References

Cameron, S. J., & Orr, R. R. (1991). Parents' perceptions of professionals when their child has a developmental disability. *Guidance and Counseling, 6*(5), 43–50.

Darling, R. B. (1988). Parental entrepreneurship: A consumerist response to professional dominance. *Journal of Social Issues, 44*(1), 141–158.

Dunst, C. J., Trivette, C. M., & Lapointe, N. (1994). Meaning and key characteristics of empowerment. In C. J. Dunst, C. M. Trivette, & A. G. Deal (Eds.). (1994). *Supporting and strengthening families.* (pp. 12–29) Cambridge, MA: Brookline Books.

Fish, M. C. (1995). Best practices in working with parents of children with disabilities. In A. Thomas & J. Grimes (Eds.), *Best practices in school psychology* (3rd ed., pp. 1061–1070). Bethesda, MD: National Association of School Psychologists.

Freud, S. (1966). *Introductory lectures on psycho-analysis.* (J. Strachey, Trans). New York: W. W. Norton & Co. (Original work published 1920.)

Glazer, A. (2014). Communication matters: Effective oral communication of evaluation results. *Communique, 42*(6). Retrieved from www.nasponline.org

Goleman, D. (1995). *Emotional intelligence: Why it can matter more than IQ*. New York, NY: Bantam Books.

Huebner, E. S. (1992). Leadership skills for school psychologists: Improving parental involvement in multi-disciplinary team interactions. In S. Christenson & J. Close Conoley (Eds.), *Home-school collaboration: Enhancing children's academic and social competence* (pp. 409–422). Bethesda, MD: National Association of School Psychologists.

Jung, C. J. (1933). *Modern man in search of a soul*. (W. S. Dell & C. F. Baynes, Trans). New York: Harcourt.

Kroth, R. L. (1985). *Communicating with parents of exceptional children*. (2nd ed.). Denver, CO: Love Publishing.

Mather, N., & Wendling, B. J. (2014). *Woodcock Johnson IV Tests of Cognitive Abilities Examiner's Manual*. Rolling Meadows, IL: Riverside.

Nichols, M. P. & Davis, S. (2016). *Family therapy concepts and methods* (11th ed.). Upper Saddle River, NJ: Pearson.

Phillips, E. (2008). When parents aren't enough: External advocacy in special education. *Yale Law Journal, 117*(8), 1802–1853.

Pollak, J. M. (1988). The feedback process with parents in child and adolescent psychological assessment. *Psychology in the Schools, 25*, 143–153.

Pruitt, P., Wandry, D., & Hollums, D. (1998). Listen to us! Parents speak out about their interactions with special educators. *Preventing School Failure, 42*(4), 161–167.

Reynolds, C. R., & Livingston, R. B. (2014). A psychometric primer for school psychologists. In P. Harrison & A. Thomas (Eds.), *Best practices in school psychology: Foundations* (pp. 281–300). Bethesda, MD: National Association of School Psychologists.

Sachs-Wise, P. (1995). Communicating with parents. In A. Thomas & J. Grimes (Eds.), *Best practices in school psychology* (3rd ed., pp. 661–666). Bethesda, MD: National Association of School Psychologists.

Sattler, J. M. (2018). *Assessment of children: Cognitive foundations and applications* (6th ed.). La Mesa, CA: Jerome M. Sattler.

Seligman, M., & Darling, R. B. (1997). *Ordinary families, special children*. New York, NY: Guilford Press.

Teyber, E. & Teyber, F. H. (2017). *Interpersonal process in therapy: An integrative model* (7th ed.). Boston, MA: Cengage Learning.

Tharinger, D. J., Finn, S. E., Hersh, B., Wilkinson, A., Christopher, G. B., & Tran, A. (2008). Assessment feedback with parents and preadolescent children: A collaborative approach. *Professional Psychology: Research and Practice, 39*(6), 600–609.

Vickers, H. S., Minke, K. M., & Anderson, K. J. (2002). Best practices in facilitating collaborative family-teacher routine conferences. In A. Thomas & J. Grimes (Eds.), *Best practices in school psychology* (4th ed., pp. 431–449). Bethseda, MD: Author.

Wechsler, D. (2014). *WISC-V: Technical and interpretive manual*. San Antonio, TX: Pearson.

6 Creating a Permanent Product with the Parent
Utilizing the Feedback Model

The purpose of the Feedback Model is to create a snapshot of the evaluation results that parents can later use to better understand the detailed psychological report. The Feedback Model provides parents with the prerequisite content knowledge to understanding their child's performance within the context of the assessment setting utilizing specific methods and instruments. Chapter 6 builds upon information discussed in the earlier chapters and presents the specific steps to the Feedback Model with their accompanying rationale.

Note that use of the psycho-educational report of the evaluation during the feedback process is avoided. The psycho-educational report serves as a legal document that is highly detailed, technical, and likely confusing to the parent. As such, the practitioner should avoid reading the report verbatim to parents at all costs during the feedback process because this practice might be perceived to be condescending in nature to the parent and it can potentially exasperate parent anxiety and confusion in the moment. Instead of using the psycho-educational report during the feedback process, the practitioner utilizing the Feedback Model creates a permanent product of the evaluation results in the presence of the parent. Parents then can use this permanent product to better understand the evaluation results when they are reading the psycho-educational report at a later (and less stressful) time.

Also note that practitioners will need to adapt the verbiage at some steps of the Feedback Model in order to accurately reflect the assessment procedures utilized during the evaluation. For example, at Step 5 of the Feedback Model, the practitioner is to provide a broad overview of the evaluation and set an agenda through stating the following,

> During the time with [child's name], we measured his or her overall cognitive functioning or how smart he or she is; academic skills in reading, math, and oral and written language; visual motor functioning; collected behavioral ratings from you, the teacher, and [student's name]; reviewed information provided by you and his teacher; and collected observations from the classroom and evaluation setting. The goal of this process is to take all of this information and sift through it … identifying learning strengths and challenges and then looking to see what types of recommendations would be most appropriate.

The practitioner will need to adjust this verbiage if a particular domain was not assessed for some reason, observations did not occur in multiple settings (i.e. classroom), or data were not obtained from a targeted source (i.e. parent, teacher, student).

Step 1: Host

This step is intended to begin with the initial parent-practitioner interaction immediately prior to beginning the formal feedback meeting. At this time, the practitioner greets the parent, initiates small-talk with the parent about neutral topics, and accompanies parent into the meeting setting.

Rationale

The amount of stress and anxiety experienced by the parent in the time leading up to the feedback meeting cannot be overstated. Remember that parent expectations of the meeting are likely directly related to their past educational experiences, experiences with mental health providers, and past and present communications with the school. Furthermore, their expectations may be shadowed by experiences that occurred immediately prior to the meeting, such as enduring traffic and parking headaches en route to the meeting or witnessing a hostile interaction between a student and office staff member while waiting for the feedback meeting to begin. Thus, it is prudent for the practitioner to assume that the parent is not necessarily relaxed at the time of the feedback meeting.

At Step 1, the practitioner's goal is to actively "join" with the parent and (re) establish rapport. The practitioner should introduce himself or herself and initiate neutral conversation with the parent to open the communication loop. Examples of neutral conversation starters include the weather, the busyness of the waiting-room setting, and recent holiday-breaks. During this initial conversation, the practitioner should appear to be pleasant and agreeable while providing the parent with ample opportunity to speak. As the parent shares information, the practitioner then shares the names of the others who are participating in the feedback meeting while accompanying the parent into the meeting room. The practitioner introduces the parent when entering the room and then seats himself or herself at the table next to the parent. Being seated alongside the parent, instead of across the table, nonverbally communicates support rather than authority over the parent and it will be easier for the practitioner to illustrate or draw-out the evaluation results during the later steps of the Feedback Model.

Step 2: Point Out One Unique Attribute of the Child

When it is time for the practitioner to begin sharing results of the comprehensive psycho-educational evaluation, he or she immediately begins by genuinely stating a unique attribute of the child. This attribute should describe a characteristic of the child as a person, rather than a student. For example, a practitioner might state the following, "[the student] and I worked together for many hours across several days and I need to say that she has one of the most likeable sense-of-humor that I have encountered." Alternatively, the practitioner might comment on a student interest or skill, such as "[the student] and I worked together for many hours across several days and I need to say that she is really proud of knowing the lyrics to all of those Bay City Rollers' songs." After sharing such comments, most parents will use the opportunity to further talk about the child and share additional details. However, some parents may be reluctant to speak and with these cases the practitioner is encouraged to ask the follow-up question, "Is this how you see [the student] at home?"

In some cases, particularly when evaluating for significant social-emotional and behavior concerns, the student may have been noncompliant with the examiner leading to a grueling evaluation experience. With these cases, the practitioner still needs to share a unique attribute about the child, but he or she must gently do so while implying some challenges to avoid being untruthful to the parent. For example, regarding a child who was noncompliant during the evaluation process, the practitioner might state, "[the student] and I worked together for many hours across several days and I need to say that she really made me earn my pay … [the student] required consistent redirection and prompting to remain on-task … is this how you see her at home?" The practitioner would make this statement to the parent if the child was challenging to work with during the evaluation, behavioral rating scale results suggested that these challenges are persistent across the settings, and an outcome of the evaluation was a recommendation for the educational diagnosis of Emotional Disturbance.

Rationale

As reviewed in previous chapters, parents have criticized special education teams for not recognizing the individuality of their child beyond a specific case number. This step explicitly demonstrates to the parent that the practitioner has taken time to become familiar with the child and that his or her attributes were meaningful enough to warrant specific comment. This step also provides the practitioner with the opportunity to introduce significant social-emotional behavioral difficulties of the child if he or she demonstrated challenging behaviors while working with the practitioner. In the latter, it is best to recognize these behaviors early in the feedback process, gradually comment on them as feedback proceeds, and then discuss the behaviors in more depth when reviewing the results of the social-emotional and behavioral rating scales. Doing so prepares the parent in increments and helps to avoid an adverse parent reaction when the final educational diagnosis is recommended.

Step 3: Ask the Parent, "What Did Your Child Think of the Evaluation Process?"

Contrary to popular belief, children regularly communicate information to their parent about their school day whether it be through a verbal or nonverbal medium. In some instances, depending on the developmental level of the child and the degree to which he or she has been exposed to parent-talk about the school, the child's communications about school may be presented in a manner to align with parent perceptions; thus, creating a dysfunctional home-school triangle when the parent is already angry at the school. A dysfunctional home-school triangle is toxic to effective home-school partnerships and it occurs when students and parents align in an effort to attack or defend themselves against the school (Christensen & Conoley, 1992). As a side note, a healthy home-school triangle exists when parents and the school align to educate the child within established rules, boundaries, and expectations.

After commenting on a unique attribute of the child, the practitioner directly asks the parent, "What did your child think of the evaluation process?" The parent's response then provides the practitioner with a window of opportunity to learn if a dysfunctional home-school triangle exists. If the parent describes the child's experience as neutral or positive, then the practitioner should proceed with the feedback as planned, taking reasonable calculated risks and sharing the results in a straightforward and understandable manner. Alternatively, if the parent shares that the child's experience was negative, the practitioner should listen attentively and proceed more cautiously when sharing evaluation results that might be inconsistent with parent expectations to avoid an adverse parent response.

On some occasions, when asked "What did your child think of the evaluation process?" parents might shrug their shoulders and simply state "Nothing." At this time, practitioners might offer a simple face-saver and respond as follows,

> Its ok if [name of student] didn't say anything to you about the evaluation, I typically ask because it is interesting to hear how children describe the process to their parents … you would be amazed at the stories that I have heard throughout the years.

Rationale

A common criticism parents have of home-school meetings is that they are not given opportunity to talk. Through asking this simple question, parents are provided an explicit opportunity to share information during the feedback process while the practitioner obtains insight regarding the parent's potential resistance to the evaluation results.

Step 4: State the Purpose of the Feedback Meeting

Depending on family size, daily stressors, and hectic schedules, a parent may show up to attend the feedback meeting without actually knowing of the meeting's true purpose. Furthermore, the parent may also have expectations of the feedback meeting based on prior experiences with previous evaluations and special education team meetings. Thus, it is necessary for the practitioner to state the following.

> The purpose of this meeting is for us to provide you with a "snapshot" of [student's name] performance and results documented in the

psycho-educational evaluation report that you will receive (or already have received) that you can read at your leisure.

Rationale

This step helps to establish the scope and manage the parent's expectations of the meeting while communicating that the meeting time will be dedicated to better understand his or her child's performance on the evaluation rather than reviewing the intricacies of the complex psycho-educational report. This step is intended to empower the parent, recognizing that he or she has the capacity to understand the evaluation process, results, and recommendations when provided with the appropriate tools.

Step 5: Provide a Broad Overview of the Evaluation and Set an Agenda

As reviewed in previous chapters, it is essential for the parent to be provided with a verbal agenda at the start of the meeting. An agenda aids in reducing the parent's anxiety, as it helps the parent to predict the immediate future. The practitioner provides a broad overview of the evaluation and establishes an agenda through stating the following.

> During the time with [child's name], we measured his or her overall cognitive functioning or how smart he or she is; academic skills in reading, math, and oral and written language; visual motor functioning; collected behavioral ratings from you, the teacher, and [student's name]; reviewed information provided by you and his teacher; and collected observations from the classroom and evaluation setting. The goal of this process is to take all of this information and sift through it … identifying learning strengths and challenges and then looking to see what types of recommendations would be most appropriate.

Rationale

In addition to establishing an agenda, this step reminds the parent of his or her participation in the evaluation; thus, giving the parent a degree of ownership in the results, conclusions, and recommendations. With this ownership, the parent is part of the process; thereby reducing the likelihood of potential conflict with the conclusions and recommendations. This step also emphasizes the multimodal and multi-factored nature of the evaluation- a best-practices characteristic stressed in the federal regulations (Federal Register, 2006; Sattler, 2018).

Step 6: Provide an Overview of Standardized Assessment

This step builds upon Step 5, clarifying the nature of the evaluation process and giving the parent the necessary background information to better understand the results when presented. The practitioner states the following at this step.

When we conduct comprehensive evaluations with students, we compare the student's individual performance to others of similar age in the standardization sample. The standardization sample being a group of other children of similar age throughout the United States who have completed the same measures. When we do this comparison, performance is then classified into different ranges.

Rationale

Considering that it takes years of specialized training and supervision in the administration, scoring, and interpretation of standardized measures, one cannot expect a parent to immediately grasp the intricacies of norm referenced assessment. As such, the parent then by default draws from his or her previous knowledge of "testing," which probably involves classroom-based exams that are typically scored based on percentage correct (0–100%) criterion. This step helps to shape the parent's expectation of feedback, informing the parent from the onset that the evaluation results are described in terms of ranges rather than through the 0–100 percent metric.

Step 7: Draw the Graph

As described at the beginning of this chapter, the Feedback Model deemphasizes use of the psycho-educational report while reviewing the evaluation results with the parent. Because the psycho-educational report is lengthy, complex, and filled with technical terminology, it could become a distraction to the parent when the practitioner is attempting to review the evaluation results, as the parent may actively be reading the report and/or become fixated with terminology. If the parent arrives with the psycho-educational report in hand at the feedback meeting, the practitioner should direct the parent to set the report aside at this time while assuring that "the results will be reviewed in a simpler and clearer manner." Note that the practitioner is encouraged to work from tables of scores from the report, rather than the entire report, at this time. These tables of scores should be committed to memory, or be placed on the practitioner's lap, to avoid enticing the parent with a potential distraction.

At Step 7, the practitioner draws a horizontal line graph on a blank sheet of paper (landscape), labeling the left margin with the descriptive classifications of ranges while explaining what performance in each range entails. This process requires the practitioner to draw from the prerequisite skills and knowledge (*Descriptive Categories of Standardized Scores*) reviewed in Chapter 5.

Rationale

Without referring to the psycho-educational report, the practitioner is beginning to create a permanent product of the evaluation results in the presence of the parent. This practice helps to improve the credibility of the practitioner in the eyes of the parent, as it communicates the practitioner's expertise with the assessment

Figure 6.1 Sample Plot of Results

process and his or her individual knowledge of the child. Consider the following example.

You take your car to the shop for repair because it is not properly working and you do not know the cause. When you pick your car up after the repair, the attendant shares the cost and provides you with a pamphlet of the services completed. You glance at the pamphlet to try to better understand the costs, reluctantly pay the bill, and leave the shop questioning if the services were really provided and the technicians were truly qualified. Now, using the same example, think of how your reaction to the experience may differ. Instead of talking with the attendant, the technician briefly meets with you and "draws-out" the services that were completed, explains why the services were necessary, and shows you the parts that were replaced. Chances are that you leave the shop much more satisfied with services from the second example rather than the first. With the second example, you spoke with the individual who actually completed the repair work, examined the faulty part, and learned about the repair process from the technician in a direct and concrete manner. Because the second example demystified the repair process, you are likely more trusting of their services and will return in the future. This same principle is applied to feedback meetings with parents. In the vast majority of instances, if the parent deems the practitioner to be credible and trustworthy, and the evaluation results and conclusions are reviewed in a clear and understandable manner, then the parent is likely to be satisfied with the services obtained and agreeable towards the outcome of the evaluation.

During Step 7, the practitioner is also providing the parent with operational definitions of the descriptive range classifications. Doing so increases transparency and gives meaning to the descriptive categories, as the parent is better able to qualitatively understand performance at different levels.

Step 8: Explain the Caveats to Ranges and Interpretations

After the graph with the descriptive ranges is drawn in the presence of the parent, the practitioner shares general information about the descriptive ranges and score interpretations with the parent. At this time, caution is needed in order to avoid overloading the parent's short-term working memory capacity. Thus, the practitioner should provide the parent with a sufficient amount of information to understand typical evaluation profiles and state the following.

> As we look at this graph, the vast majority of students' skills fall between the High Average and Low Average Ranges … it is the way that the instruments are designed. As we move further away from the middle ranges, skills become further above or below what we would expect given a student's age. It is not typical to have skills equally developed and in one range across all of the domains evaluated. Students are usually strong in one area and not so strong in another. We become most concerned when skills fall in the Very Low Range or below, indicating underdeveloped skills and abilities.

Rationale

Providing an explanation of the graph and general score interpretation helps to shape the parent's expectations of the evaluation results and normalize reasonable variability in his or her child's performance. From a larger perspective, this step is essentially supplying the parent with the tools to understand intra and inter individual differences in performance before his or her child's skills are graphed.

Step 9: Describe Structure of Cognitive Instrument

After drawing the table, explaining the ranges, and providing basic information regarding score interpretation, the practitioner then draws out, on the reverse side of the paper or on another blank sheet, the factor structure of the cognitive instrument while explaining the types of tasks that make up each factor score. This process requires the practitioner to utilize the prerequisite skills and knowledge (*Common Constructs Measured During the Evaluation-Intelligence/Cognitive Functioning*) reviewed in Chapter 5 and describe the cognitive constructs while drawing. Using the Woodcock-Johnson Tests of Cognitive Abilities-Fourth Edition as an example, the practitioner states the following at Step 9 of the Feedback Model. Note that brief subtest descriptions are provided when describing each domain.

> When measuring a student's cognitive functioning, or how smart he or she is, the instruments that we use typically yield a broad overall score and composite scores in various areas. The composite scores help us to better understand the overall performance and they represent performance in the

Comprehension-Knowledge, Fluid Reasoning, Cognitive Processing Speed, and Short-term working-memory domains. The Comprehension-Knowledge domain measures the amount of information that [the student] has acquired through language and it required [the student] to generate antonyms and synonyms to words of increasing difficulty; and respond to "what" and "where" questions. The Fluid Reasoning domain examined [the student's] problem solving skills, or ability "to think on his or her feet" and required [the student] to determine the rule when presented with a complete stimulus set; and to state the missing number in a series of numbers. The Cognitive Processing Speed domain measured [the student's] ability to quickly perform both simple and complex cognitive tasks with controlled attention under timed conditions and required [the student] to identify two identical letter patterns in a row of patterns. The Short-Term Working-Memory domain measured [the student's] ability to apprehend and hold information in immediate awareness and then use or manipulate the information to carry-out a necessary goal. This domain required [the student] to hold a span of numbers in memory and perform a mental operation by reversing the sequence of numbers; and listen to an intermingled series of animals and digits presented on an audio recording and answer specific question regarding the sequence.

Figures 6.2 and Figure 6.3 provide sample illustrations of Woodcock-Johnson Tests of Cognitive Abilities-Fourth Edition standard battery (McGrew, LaForte, & Shrank, 2014) and the primary index scores of Wechsler Intelligence Scale for Children-Fifth Edition (Wechsler, 2014), respectively. Note that a similar method of drawing out other popular measures, such as the Stanford-Binet Intelligence Scales-Fifth Edition and the Differential Ability Scales-Second Edition, would apply (Elliott, 2007; Roid, 2003).

Rationale

Comprehensive psycho-educational evaluations typically yield an overall level of cognitive/intellectual functioning. Although this overall score is believed to be required for most eligibility decisions, it is limited in terms of its utility in explaining performance in specific academic domains. Thus, it is necessary that the practitioner provide the parent with an explanation of the broad cognitive composite and its related composite or factor scores. With this explanation, the parent learns that there are multiple cognitive constructs underlying a student's ability, not simply an "IQ score."

Step 10: Plot the Overall Cognitive Score and Factor Scores in Appropriate Ranges

After fully reviewing the factor structure of the cognitive instrument, the practitioner returns to the original graph with the descriptive ranges to plot the overall level of cognitive functioning and subsequent composite or factor scores. Begin at the far left side of the graph, plot the overall cognitive score, and then state the

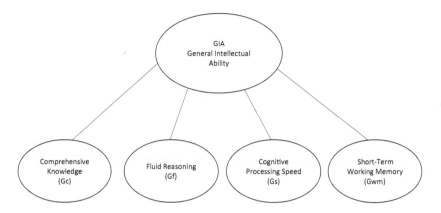

Figure 6.2 Sample Illustration of the Woodcock-Johnson-Fourth Edition: Test of Cognitive
Ability: Standard Battery

Source: McGraw, Laforte, & Shrank, 2014

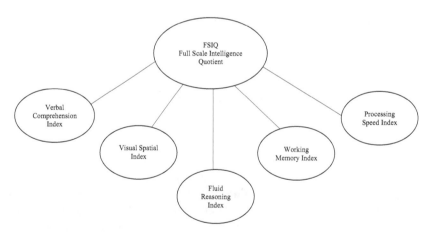

Figure 6.3 Sample Illustration of the Wechsler Intelligence Scale for Children-Fifth Edition:
Primary Index Scores

Source: Wechsler, 2014

range in which it falls (Figure 6.4). Then proceed with each composite or factor
score, individually plotting each score while moving to the right and stating the
range in which the score falls. Use an abbreviation to represent each domain
name. Describe any unusual subtest performance while plotting the related factor
score. Plot unusual subtest performance in the same column as the factor score
(Figure 6.5). Otherwise, refrain from reviewing each individual subtest to avoid
overloading the parent's short-term working memory capacity.

Figure 6.4 Plot of Overall Level of Cognitive Functioning

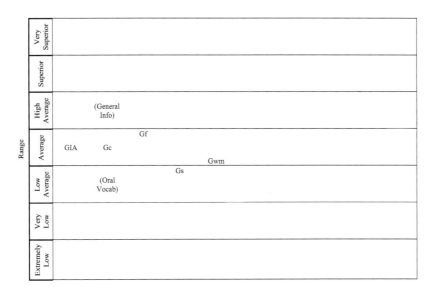

Figure 6.5 Plot of Overall Level of Cognitive Functioning with Factor Scores and Unusual Subtest Performance

Rationale

The purpose of Step 10 is to show the parent where the child's performance is on the graph before he or she hears of the results. This process makes the abstract nature of inter and intra performance comparisons more concrete and easy to understand for the parent. It also helps to alleviate any hesitation on behalf of the practitioner when describing performance that may cause the parent to have an adverse emotional reaction, as the parent sees the level of performance before hearing the practitioner provide a description.

The Feedback Model intentionally begins with explaining the cognitive results for two reasons. First, cognitive functioning has underlying and inherent relationships to other domains measured in the comprehensive psycho-educational evaluation. Thus, it can serve as a reference point when describing the results of academic and visual–motor measures and explaining social-emotional and behavioral difficulties. Next, through explaining the cognitive results first, the parent is immediately able to answer his or her primary and often unspoken concern, "Is my child smart enough to be successful in school?" Delaying a response to this question would likely create anxiety and be a distraction for the parent throughout the feedback session.

Step 11: Describe the Structure of Achievement Instrument

On the reverse side of the graph or another blank sheet, the practitioner draws out the factor structure of the achievement instrument while explaining the types of tasks that make up each factor score. This process requires the practitioner to utilize the prerequisite skills and knowledge (*Common Constructs Measured During the Evaluation-Academic Functioning*) reviewed in Chapter 5 and to describe the academic constructs while drawing. Using the Woodcock-Johnson Tests of Achievement-Fourth Edition as an example, the practitioner states the following at Step 11 of the Feedback Model. Note that brief subtest descriptions are provided when describing each domain.

> When measuring a student's academic functioning, the instruments used typically yield an overall achievement score, and broad composite scores in the areas of reading, mathematics, and written language. The Broad Reading domain measured [the student's] word decoding, reading comprehension, and reading fluency skills; and it required [the student] to read word lists of increasing difficulty, read a short passage and generate a missing word that makes sense in the passage, and read simple sentences and decide if the statement is true or false by circling Yes or No. The Broad Mathematics domain measured [the student's] math calculation, application, and fluency ability; and it required [the student] to perform mathematical calculations of increasing difficulty, listen to a problem and decide on the appropriate mathematical operation to use; and complete a series of simple arithmetic problems in a 3-minute time frame. The Written Language domain measured [the student's] spelling skills and ability to write meaningful sentences when given prompts; and it required [the student] to spell words of increasing difficulty dictated by the

examiner, formulate and write simple sentences using 3 provided words in a 5-minute time-frame, and write quality sentences in response to prompts of increasing difficulty.

Figures 6.6 and Figure 6.7 provide sample illustrations of Woodcock-Johnson Tests of Achievement-Fourth Edition (Schrank, Mather, & McGrew, 2014) and the

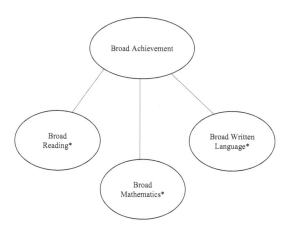

Figure 6.6 Sample Illustration of the Woodcock-Johnson Tests of Achievement-Fourth Edition

Note:
* Broad Achievement composites are described, as each contain subtests that are included in related cluster scores (i.e. Basic Reading Skills, Math Calculation Skills, and Written Language.)

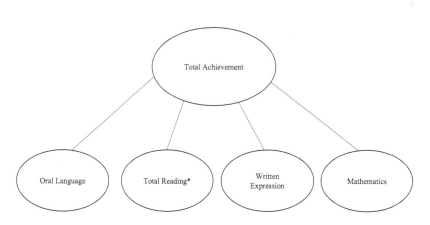

Figure 6.7 Sample Illustration of the Wechsler Individual Achievement Test-Third-Edition

Note:
* The Total Reading Composite Score is described, as it incorporates the subtests of the Basic Reading and Reading Comprehension and Fluency Composites

Wechsler Individual Achievement Test-Third Edition (Wechsler, 2005), respectively. Note that a similar method of drawing-out other popular measures, such as the Kaufman Test of Educational Achievement-Third Edition would apply (Kaufman & Kaufman, 2014).

Rationale

The parent obtains an understanding of the various achievement domains measured and recognizes that these domains are slightly different than traditional academic subjects (English, science, social studies, geometry).

Step 12: Plot the Overall Achievement Score and Factor Scores in Appropriate Ranges

After fully reviewing the factor structure of the achievement measure, the practitioner returns to the original graph to plot the overall level of achievement and subsequent composite or factor scores. Begin alongside the last cognitive score indicated, plot the overall achievement score, and then state the range in which it falls (Figure 6.8). Then proceed with each composite or factor score, individually plotting each score while moving to the right and stating the range in which the score falls. Use an abbreviation to represent each academic skill area. Describe any unusual subtest performance while plotting the related factor score. Plot unusual subtest performance in the same column as the factor score (Figure 6.9). Otherwise, refrain from reviewing each individual subtest to avoid overloading the parent's short-term working memory capacity. After the performance on the

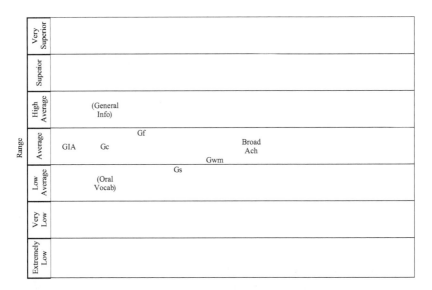

Figure 6.8 Plot of Overall Cognitive Functioning and Broad Achievement

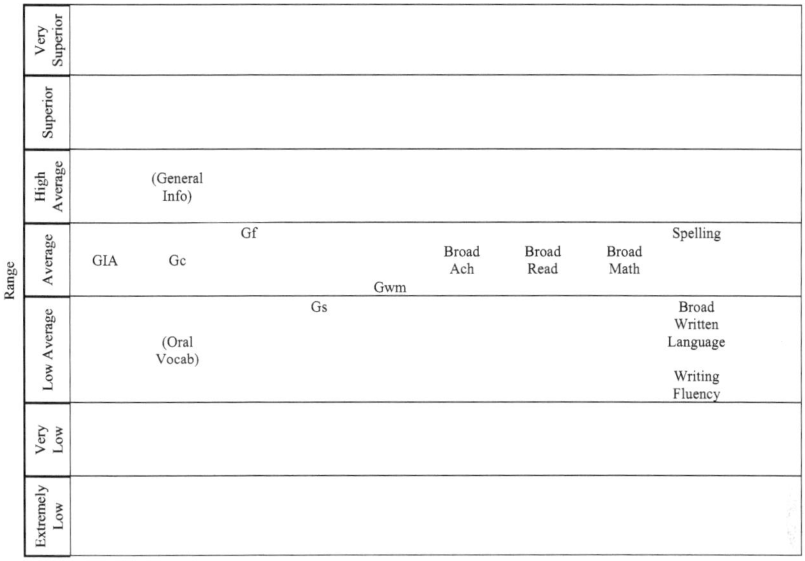

Range							
Very Superior							
Superior							
High Average	(General Info)						
Average	GIA Gc	Gf		Broad Ach	Broad Read	Broad Math	Spelling
			Gwm				
Low Average	(Oral Vocab)	Gs					Broad Written Language Writing Fluency
Very Low							
Extremely Low							

Figure 6.9 Plot of Overall Cognitive Functioning, Broad Achievement, and Achievement Domains with Unusual Achievement Subtest Performance

achievement measure is plotted in its entirety, comment on the overall pattern of results. Indicate if the overall oral language, reading, written language, and mathematics skills are developed at a level that is generally consistent with cognitive ability while recognizing that most students' performance vary across the cognitive and academic domains.

Rationale

The purpose of Step 12 is similar to that of Step 10. With the parent already familiar with the descriptive ranges, the practitioner shows the parent where the child's academic skills are on the graph before he or she hears of the results. This process makes the abstract nature of inter and intra performance comparisons more concrete and easy to understand for the parent. It also helps to alleviate any hesitation on behalf of the practitioner when describing performance that may cause the parent to have an adverse emotional reaction, as the parent sees the level of performance before hearing the practitioner provide a description.

Step 13: Plot the Curriculum Based-Measure (CBM) Results (if Applicable)

A comprehensive psycho-educational evaluation would include curriculum-based measures (CBM) in keeping with a best-practices approach, as CBM results provide valuable and authentic data regarding the student's raw academic skills.

However, it is recognized that this practice many times is not followed for a variety of reasons, particularly if the comprehensive psycho-educational evaluation is for a high-school age student or it is completed in a private, rather than school-based setting.

With popular CBM measures, such as AIMSWEB and DIBELS, results are typically reported in a "task-by-time" manner and assigned a percentile rank. For example, on a CBM oral reading fluency measure, a student's performance is described in terms of words read correctly per minute and assigned a percentile rank. The percentile rank denotes the student's performance compared to others of similar grade. Using the following percentile rank descriptions, the practitioner can then loosely associate the CBM results to performance in the related area on the standardized norm referenced measure of achievement.

- Percentile Rank < 25: Underdeveloped skills compared to similar grade peers.
- Percentile Rank between 25 and 49: Skills slightly below similar grade peers.
- Percentile Rank between 50 and 75: Skills consistent with similar grade peers.
- Percentile Rank > 75: Skills above similar grade peers.

Consider the following example. A student earned a Broad Reading score in the Average Range on the WJ-IV Achievement and performance on a CBM oral reading fluency measure was at the 55th percentile rank. With this example, the CBM results are consistent with performance in the reading domain on the WJ-IV Achievement. Using another example, a student earned a Broad Reading score in the High Average Range on the WJ-IV Achievement and performance on the CBM oral reading fluency measure was at the 30th percentile rank. In this case, the CBM results are inconsistent with performance in the Broad Reading domain of the WJ-IV Achievement.

At Step 13 of the Feedback Model, the practitioner explains the basic CBM procedures, shares the "task-by-time" results, and then translates the percentile rank into terms of being consistent or inconsistent with performance in the relative achievement domain. This performance is then plotted alongside the related domain of the achievement measure. See Figure 6.10.

Rationale

CBM results add substance to a comprehensive psycho-educational evaluation, as they yield authentic data regarding a student's academic skills that can be quickly utilized to develop a specific intervention. Through plotting the results alongside of student's performance on the related achievement measure, the multi-modal and multi-factor nature of the evaluation is confirmed to the parent and the parent is better able to observe intra and inter performance variations of the student.

Step 14: Plot Visual Motor Results (if Applicable)

Similar to CBM, including a measure of visual motor functioning as part of the assessment procedures supports a best-practices approach in conducting a

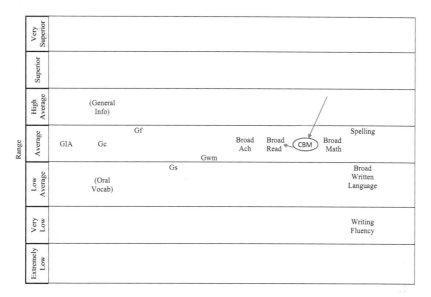

Figure 6.10 Plot of Overall Cognitive and Academic Functioning with CBM Results

multi-modal and multi-factor evaluation. The practitioner needs to assess in all domains related to the referral question(s) and rule out sensory–motor issues as a contributing factor to potential learning and/or behavioral issues. However, it is recognized that this practice does not always occur depending on the structure and responsibilities of the special education evaluation team, as visual–motor assessment might be an assigned duty of the occupational therapist. If the practitioner includes a measure of visual motor functioning in the comprehensive psycho-educational evaluation, then it is recommended that he or she avoids over-interpreting the results and instead utilizes the data to establish whether or not visual–motor functioning adversely affected the evaluation results across the domains measured. Visual–motor assessment in its purest form falls within the skill-set of a credentialed occupational therapist and a student with significant visual-motor difficulties should be referred to this professional for further evaluation.

At Step 14 of the Feedback Model, the practitioner describes the visual-motor assessment and then plots the results on the graph alongside of the achievement (Figure 6.11). This process requires the practitioner to utilize the prerequisite skills and knowledge (*Common Constructs Measured During the Evaluation-Visual-Motor Skills*) reviewed in Chapter 5 and to state the following while plotting performance on the graph.

Comprehensive psycho-educational evaluations commonly include a measure of visual-motor functioning to help identify if visual-motor skills adversely affected a student's performance the overall evaluation. To do so, students are usually required to draw increasingly complex geometric figures without

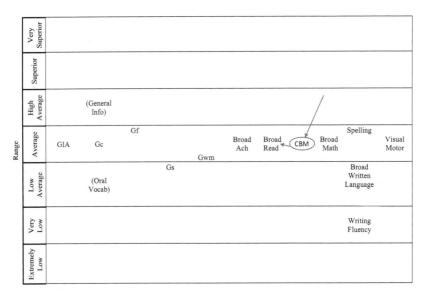

Figure 6.11 Plot of Overall Cognitive and Academic Functioning, CBM Results, and Visual-Motor Skills

erasing. Performance on visual-motor tasks lets us know if students can accurately recreate information presented to them visually. [The student's] overall visual-motor functioning was measured in the [state Range] and at a level [above, below, consistent, generally consistent] with what would be expected given his or her age.

Rationale

Parents see the visual motor results plotted alongside of the student's performance in the cognitive and academic domains. The graph now provides parents with a visual representation of the evaluation results that most directly help to explain the student's performance in the classroom setting.

Step 15: Review of Social-Emotional and Behavioral Results

Social-emotional and behavioral evaluation is complex and often overwhelming to graduate trainees and early career practitioners because of the large amount of data collected and its need to be adequately synthesized. A best-practices approach to evaluating social-emotional and behavioral functioning occurs through parent, teacher, and self-report interviews; observations collected from the evaluation and classroom settings; and rating scales completed by multiple-respondents (i.e. parent, teacher, and student). It is recognized that the practitioner may be unable to collect all of these data in daily practice because of an overloaded schedule and noncompliance on behalf of parents and teachers. However, to sufficiently evaluate social-emotional and behavioral functioning at minimum, the evaluation should include observation data collected from multiple settings and interview and rating scale data from the student and one other adult.

At Step 15 of the Feedback Model, the practitioner discusses his or her synthesis of the social-emotional and behavioral data rather than systematically reviewing the results from each individual data source. This practice is a necessity in order to avoid overloading the parent's short-term working memory. During this discussion, the graph of the cognitive, achievement, and visual-motor results remains in front of the parent and the practitioner reviews clinical and at-risk ratings that are supported by confirming data collected through the interviews and observations. This process requires the practitioner to utilize the prerequisite skills and knowledge (*Common Constructs Measured During the Evaluation-Social-Emotional Functioning*) reviewed in Chapter 5. The first example of verbiage below explains social-emotional and behavioral results within a typical or normal range; and the second example is more appropriately applied to cases with significant issues.

> [The student's] social-emotional and behavioral functioning was evaluated through observations in the classroom setting and while working with the examiner; and parent, student, and teacher interviews and rating scales. When we look at all of these data collected, we see that [student's name] overall level of social-emotional and behavioral functioning is consistent with what would be expected given his or her age. Based on the information collected, [the student] appears to get-along-well with peers and adults, follows rules, and controls his or her emotional reactions to a degree that is typical for his or her age. Significant internalizing or externalizing behavioral difficulties were not noted.

> [The student's] social-emotional and behavioral functioning was evaluated through observations in the classroom setting and while working with the examiner; and parent, student, and teacher interviews and rating scales. When we look at all of these data collected, we see that [student's name] overall level of social-emotional and behavioral functioning is inconsistent with what would be expected given his or her age. Clinically significant ratings were obtained in domains measuring [state domains]. At-risk ratings were also obtained in areas measuring [state domains]. These ratings are supported by interview and observation data, as [indicate source- parent, teacher, student] also reported similar behaviors and these behaviors were observed in the [indicate setting].

If significant social-emotional and behavioral difficulties are evident from the comprehensive psycho-educational evaluation, the practitioner then refers the parent to the graph of the cognitive, achievement, and visual-motor results and explains how the behaviors are impeding the student's performance in the academic setting. Assuming that the student's cognitive and academic skills are at least within a Low Average Range and no specific learning disabilities are indicated, sample verbiage for this process is as follows.

> Looking back at [the student's] learning potential and academic skills, we see that [the student] has the potential to be successful in the school setting; however, behaviors are interfering with his or her receptiveness towards instruction in the typical school environment.

Rationale

Results of the social-emotional and behavioral component of the assessment are discussed while the pattern of performance across the cognitive, academic, and visual-motor domains is visually documented in front of the parent. With these results depicted in front of the parent, he or she is likely to have greater short-term working-memory capacity to process the complex and often delicate conversation regarding social-emotional and behavioral functioning. Note that the social-emotional and behavioral results are described last in the Feedback Model. This decision was intentional to avoid potentially alienating the parent earlier in the feedback process, as social-emotional and behavioral results are typically related to stressors in the home environment, family dynamics, and the availability of resources to the family system.

Step 16: Conclusions and Recommendations

After reviewing the social-emotional and behavioral results, the practitioner then offers conclusions and recommendations based on the data collected. At this step, it is important for the practitioner to provide a brief rationale and to utilize the official disability category, as described by IDEA and the state's special education regulations, if an educational diagnosis is warranted. Listed below are the sample verbiage of conclusions and recommendations for: a student not eligible for a special education disability diagnosis; a student eligible for a diagnosis based on academic concerns; and a student eligible for a diagnosis because of behavioral concerns.

> Not Eligible: Based on all of the information gathered, [student's name] does not meet eligibility requirements for a special education disability category, as defined by IDEA and the [name of the state's] state special education regulations. [The student's] overall cognitive and academic functioning tested in the [name of range] and visual-motor skills were age-appropriate. Furthermore, interview, observation, and rating scale data suggested social-emotional and behavioral functioning typical for his or her age. Given this information, [the student] should [briefly state recommendations] to maintain his or her performance in the curriculum.

> Eligible due to Academic Concerns: Based on all of the information gathered, [student's name] meets eligibility requirements for [state specific disability category], as defined by IDEA and the [name of the state's] special education

regulations. [The student's] cognitive functioning tested in the [name of range] and academic skills were measured in the [state the range]. Visual-motor functioning was age-appropriate and social-emotional and behavioral concerns were not evident. Specific academic difficulties occurred in [state academic area and specifically describe underdeveloped skills]. [The student] will benefit from [briefly state recommendations] to help address his or her needs in this area.

Eligible due to Social-Emotional and Behavioral Concerns: Based on all of the information gathered, [student's name] meets eligibility requirements for [state specific disability category], as defined by IDEA and the [name of the state's] special education regulations. [The student's] overall cognitive and academic functioning tested in the [name of range] and visual-motor skills were age-appropriate. Interview, observation, and rating scale data suggested social-emotional and behavioral functioning that is inconsistent with his or her age, as [student's name] exhibits characteristics commonly associated with [indicate area; i.e. attentional difficulties, anxiety, depression, etc.]. These characteristics adversely affect his or her performance in the curriculum by [indicate how the difficulties interfere with classroom performance] and he or she will benefit from [briefly state recommendations] to help address his or her needs in this area.

Rationale

The parent is presented with the conclusions and recommendations of the psycho-educational evaluation, utilizing the specific diagnostic categories if warranted, as defined by IDEA and the state's special education guidelines. The Feedback Model prepares the parent for these conclusions and recommendations through reviewing the evaluation process and subsequent results in a structured, concrete, and transparent manner, recognizing the anxiety provoking nature of the feedback process for the parent.

Summary

Chapter 6 built upon information from previous chapters and presented the 16 steps to the Feedback Model and their accompanying rationale. The preliminary steps of the Feedback Model focus on (re)establishing rapport with the parent, emphasizing the uniqueness of the student, and establishing the purpose and agenda for the feedback meeting. Afterwards, the practitioner provides an overview of standardized assessment, draws the graph on which the results are to be plotted, and operationally defines the descriptive categories that will frame the results. The cognitive constructs measured are explained and plotted in the appropriate descriptive range and this process is repeated for the achievement measure before plotting the CBM and visual-motor results. Social-emotional and behavioral results are then discussed while the graph of the other results remains visible. The process concludes with the practitioner clearly stating the diagnostic category, if warranted, and briefly reviewing recommendations to facilitate the student's development in the academic setting. Sample verbiage was provided at many of the steps throughout the feedback process. The practitioner will need to adapt this verbiage to accurately reflect the nature of the psycho-educational evaluation and specifics of the student's performance.

References

Christenson, S. & Conoley, J. C. (Eds.). (1992). *Home-school collaboration: Enhancing children's academic and social competence.* Bethesda, MD: National Association of School Psychologists.

Elliott, C. D. (2007). *Differential Ability Scales-Second Edition: Introductory and technical handbook.* San Antonio, TX: Harcourt Assessment.

Federal Register (2006). *Part II. Department of Education: 34 CFR Parts 300 and 301. Assistance to states for the education of children with disabilities and preschool grants for children with disabilities; Final rule.* Retrieved from http://edocket.access.gpo.gov/2006/pdf/06-6656.pdf

Kaufman, A. S. & Kaufman, N. L. (2014). *Kaufman Test of Educational Achievement, Third Edition.* San Antonio, TX: Pearson.

McGrew, K. S., LaForte, E. M., & Shrank, F. A. (2014). *Woodcock-Johnson IV Technical Manual.* Rolling Meadows, IL: Riverside.

Roid, G. H. (2003). *Stanford Binet Intelligence Scales, Fifth Edition: Interpretive manual.* Itasca, IL: Riverside.

Sattler, J. M. (2018). *Assessment of children: Cognitive foundations and applications (6th ed.).* La Mesa, CA: Jerome M. Sattler.

Schrank, F.A., Mather, N., & McGrew, K. S. (2014). *Woodcock-Johnson IV Tests of Achievement.* Rolling Meadows, IL: Riverside.

Wechsler, D. (2005). *Wechsler Individual Achievement Test, Third Edition.* San Antonio, TX: Pearson.

Wechsler, D. (2014). *WISC-V: Technical and interpretive manual.* San Antonio, TX: Pearson.

7 Utilizing the Feedback Model with Diverse Populations

The school psychology profession is largely homogeneous according to a recent demographic survey, as it is composed of female practitioners in their early 40s who identify as white (Walcott, Charvet, McNamara, & Hyson, 2016). When combining this information with studies noting the disproportionality of racial and ethnic minorities receiving special education services, it seems evident that as part of their daily responsibilities, school psychology practitioners regularly complete comprehensive psycho-educational evaluations for racial and ethnic minority children (NASP, 2013; Skiba, Poloni-Staudinger, Simmons, Feggins-Azziz, & Chung, 2005). Just as these evaluations need to be carefully planned to maintain an adequate standard of validity in light of cultural factors, feedback of evaluation results with racial and ethnic minority parents must be crafted in a manner that is respectful of cultural differences and subsequent communication practices.

The current chapter provides an overview of concepts that underly delivering feedback results to racial and ethnic minority parents via the Feedback Model. Relevant APA and NASP principles of professional practice are reviewed and the construct of relational humility is presented. Afterwards, cultural humility is discussed as an alternative to cultural sensitivity and cultural competence; and the concept of micro-aggressions is presented. The chapter concludes with offering basic suggestions to practitioners and trainers to help facilitate the development of self-knowledge as an inoculation against violating the cultural perspectives of racial and ethnic minority parents during the feedback process.

Note that the current chapter intentionally takes a different tact in addressing cultural diversity when compared to other popular texts within the field (Harrison & Thomas, 2014; Sattler, 2014, 2018). The chapter focuses on broad concepts that pertain to the practitioner, rather than listing the subtle characteristics of different racial and ethnic groups. Doing so will hopefully compel the practitioner to become more introspective—critically evaluating his or her own thoughts, behaviors, and practices to better communicate with those who are different.

Principles of Professional Practice

Our professional organizations (APA, NASP) are recognized for continuously developing resources to support multi-cultural practice, divisions to organize membership, and interest groups to explore ideas. These resources help to further articulate each organization's position regarding ethically responsible service provision to diverse racial and ethnic groups. A review of APA and NASP principles that address racial, ethnic, and cultural diversity follows.

American Psychological Association

According to the APA's current Ethical Principles of Psychologists and Code of Conduct (2017), the topics of racial, ethnic, and cultural diversity are specifically described in Principle D: Justice, Principle E: Respect for People's Rights and Dignity, and Standard 3 Human Relations—Unfair Discrimination. These standards state the following (APA, 2017). Note that italics were added to each for emphasis.

Principle D: Justice

Psychologists recognize that fairness and justice entitle all persons to access to and benefit from the contributions of psychology and to *equal quality* in the processes, procedures, and services being conducted by psychologists. Psychologists exercise reasonable judgment and *take precautions to ensure that their potential biases*, the boundaries of their competence, and the limitations of their expertise do not lead to or condone unjust practices.

Principle E: Respect for People's Rights and Dignity.

Psychologists respect the dignity and worth of all people, and the rights of individuals to privacy, confidentiality, and self-determination. Psychologists are aware that special safeguards may be necessary to protect the rights and welfare of persons or communities whose vulnerabilities impair autonomous decision making. *Psychologists are aware of and respect cultural, individual, and role differences, including those based on age, gender, gender identity, race, ethnicity, culture, national origin, religion, sexual orientation, disability, language, and socioeconomic status, and consider these factors when working with members of such groups. Psychologists try to eliminate the effect on their work of biases based on those factors, and they do not knowingly participate in or condone activities of others based upon such prejudices.*

Standard 3: Human Relations- Unfair Discrimination

In their work-related activities, *psychologists do not engage in unfair discrimination based on age, gender, gender identity, race, ethnicity, culture, national origin, religion, sexual orientation, disability, socioeconomic status, or any basis proscribed by law.*

National Association of School Psychologists

NASP's Principles for Professional Ethics (2010) specifically address the topics of racial, ethnic, and cultural diversity through Principle I: Respecting the Dignity and Rights of All Persons, Principle II: Professional Competence and Responsibility, and multiple standards related to these principles. The NASP principles and standards state the following (NASP, 2010). Note that italics were added to each for emphasis.

Principle I: Respecting the Dignity and Rights of All Persons

School psychologists engage only in professional practices that *maintain the dignity of all with whom they work.* In their words and actions, school psychologists demonstrate respect for the autonomy of persons and their right to self-determination, respect for privacy, and a commitment to *just and fair treatment of all persons.*

Standard I.1.3

School psychologists ensure that an individual providing consent for school psychological services is fully informed about the nature and scope of services offered, assessment/intervention goals and procedures, any foreseeable risks, the costs of services to the parent or student (if any), and the benefits that reasonably can be expected ... *This explanation takes into account language and cultural differences, cognitive capabilities, developmental level, age, and other relevant factors so that it may be understood by the individual providing consent.*

Principle I.3 Fairness and Justice

In their words and actions, school psychologists promote fairness and justice. They use their expertise to cultivate school climates that are safe and welcoming to all persons *regardless of actual or perceived characteristics, including race, ethnicity, color, religion, ancestry, national origin, immigration status, socioeconomic status, primary language, gender, sexual orientation, gender identity, gender expression, disability, or any other distinguishing characteristics.*

Standard I.3.1

School psychologists do not engage in or condone actions or policies that discriminate against persons, *including students and their families, other recipients of service, supervisees, and colleagues based on actual or perceived characteristics including race; ethnicity; color; religion; ancestry; national origin; immigration status; socioeconomic status; primary language; gender; sexual orientation, gender identity, or gender expression; mental, physical, or sensory disability; or any other distinguishing characteristics.*

Standard I.3.2

School psychologists pursue awareness and knowledge of how diversity factors may influence child development, behavior, and school learning. In conducting psychological, educational, or behavioral evaluations or in providing interventions, therapy, counseling, or consultation services, the school psychologist takes into account individual characteristics as enumerated in Standard I.3.1 so as to provide effective services.

Standard I.3.3

School psychologists work to correct school practices that are unjustly discriminatory or that deny students, parents, or others their legal rights. They take steps to foster a school climate that is safe, accepting, and respectful of all persons.

Standard I.3.4

School psychologists strive to ensure that *all* children have equal opportunity to participate in and benefit from school programs and that *all students and families* have *access to and can benefit* from school psychological services.

Principle II.3 Responsible Assessment and Intervention Practices/Standard II.3.10

School psychologists discuss with parents the recommendations and plans for assisting their children. *This discussion takes into account the ethnic/cultural values of the family and includes alternatives that may be available.* Subsequent recommendations for program changes or additional services are discussed with parents, including any alternatives that may be available.

As suspected, APA and NASP ethical principles and standards addressing racial, ethnic, and cultural diversity are largely similar in content and verbiage. Both specifically identify protected categories of individuals and offer practitioners clear guidelines to ensure equitable practices for these populations. However, APA utilizes terminology such as "potential bias" and "prejudice"; whereas NASP seems to emphasize "discriminatory" practices. Most importantly though, the NASP principles include a specific standard that recognizes the on-going nature of developing competency in working with racial, ethnic, and culturally diverse populations, as Standard I.3.2 states that "School Psychologists pursue awareness and knowledge of how diversity factors may influence child development, behavior, and school learning" (NASP, 2010, p. 6). This standard seems to support the current trend in the multi-cultural education literature. Skill in working with racial, ethnic, and culturally diverse populations may be best developed through promoting cultural humility, a lifelong process of learning, self-reflection, and self-critique, rather than striving for the discrete endpoint of cultural competence (Tervalon & Murray-Garcia, 1998).

Relational Humility

The construct of relational humility must first be briefly reviewed to provide a context for understanding cultural humility. Relational humility falls within the domain of positive psychology and it is often discussed with other virtues such as forgiveness, gratitude, hope, optimism, and modesty (Davis, Hook, Worthington, Van Tongeren, Gartner, Jennings, & Emmons, 2011). Because of difficulty in defining the construct for research purposes, humility has been defined in terms of intra and interpersonal modesty. Intrapersonal modesty refers to having a just view of oneself that is not too high or too low; whereas, interpersonal modesty denotes the likelihood for one to regulate praise or recognition from others in a socially acceptable manner (Gregg, Hart, Sedikides, & Kumashiro, 2008). In addition to including the concepts of intra and interpersonal modesty, humility also includes prosocial interpersonal traits such as respect and empathy during conflict, openness toward different cultures and worldviews, and deference towards God or a higher power (Davis, Worthington, & Hook, 2010).

Given its name, relational humility is best understood within the context of social relationships and social roles. Relational humility, at its essence, is an orientation-towards-others and it is critical in "forming, maintaining, strengthening, and repairing social bonds" (Davis, Worthington, Hook, Emmons, Hill, Bollinger, & Van Tongeren, 2013, p. 59). Relational humility has been related to forgiveness and it is demonstrated in social relationships through avoiding superiority, showing respect, sacrificing for others, expressing empathy, and regulating self-oriented emotions in a socially acceptable manner (Davis et al., 2011). Each of these characteristics would seem essential to any human service provider, particularly those such as school psychologists, who need to have a deep understanding of students' background as part of the comprehensive psycho-educational evaluation. More importantly, these characteristics would be paramount for school psychologists in developing and maintaining a mutually respectful rapport and partnership with parents of various racial, ethnic, and cultural identities to explain evaluation results in respectful and easily understood manner.

Cultural Humility and Microaggressions

Cultural humility builds upon the construct of relational humility and it is rooted in an orientation-towards-others. Cultural humility differs from cultural competence in that cultural competence assumes a discrete end-point and it has been criticized for promoting stereotyping (Kumagai & Lypson, 2009). Cultural humility is defined as a life-long process of self-reflection and self-critique wherein one critically examines his or her own beliefs and cultural identities while learning about another's culture (Tervalon & Murray-Garcia, 1998). Thus, cultural humility requires an examination of our own background and social environment to explore how both have shaped our experience and perceptions of others. In doing so, we critically question our own assumptions, biases, and values while attempting to understand those who are racially and ethnically different. Simply stated, "we cannot understand the makeup and context of others' lives without being aware and reflective of [our] own background and situation" (Yeager & Bauer-Wu, 2013, p. 2). Thus, cultural humility plays an important role in helping to define practitioners' overall multicultural orientation.

Practitioners whose multicultural orientation is defined through cultural humility seem to have greater multicultural competence, as these individuals are less likely to commit microaggressions towards racial and ethnically diverse clients (Constantine, 2007; Hook, Farrell, Davis, DeBlaere, Van Tongeren & Utsey, 2016). Microaggressions are "brief, everyday exchanges that send denigrating messages to people of color because they belong to a racial minority group" (Sue, Capodilupo, Torino, Bucceri, Holder, Nadal, & Esquilin, 2007, p. 273). These exchanges, which can be intentional or unintentional, are often subtle and toxic, as they cause distress and remind the recipient of inequalities embedded into our social systems.

Three forms of microaggressions have been identified in the literature: microassault, microinsult, and microinvalidation (Sue et al., 2007). A microassault is an explicit, severe, and intentional denigration of an individual's racial group through name-calling, avoidant behavior or purposeful discriminatory action (Sue et al., 2007). Microassaults have been equated to deliberate "old fashioned racism" and occur through using racial epithets or deliberately attending to a White person before one of color. Alternatively, a microinsult is "characterized by communications that convey rudeness and insensitivity and demean a person's racial heritage or identity" (Sue et al., 2007, p. 274). Microinsults are "subtle snubs" that convey an insulting message, such as when a person of color is asked, "How did you get this job?" Although this question may seem innocent on a surface level, its underlying messages to a person of color might be that people of color are not qualified and the minority group member may have acquired the job through an affirmative action or quota program. Finally, microinvalidations are "characterized by communications that exclude, negate, or nullify the psychological thoughts, feelings, or experiential reality of a person of color" (Sue et al., 2007, p. 274). Examples of microinvalidation occur when individuals of color are told "we are color blind in this organization" or "we are all human" in an attempt to discredit their perceived racial and cultural experiences.

The effects of microaggressions appear to be both pervasive and extensive. Research has suggested that microaggressions can occur towards any marginalized group (i.e. individuals with disabilities, individuals with limited financial resources) and their effects can lead to a toxic and potentially harmful environment (Sue, Alsaidi, Awad, Glaeser, Calle, & Mendez, 2019). As noted in the Sue et al. (2019) article, microaggressions increase stress in the lives of marginalized populations and people of color, impede learning and problem solving, increase negative feelings and depression, and impair employee performance. More importantly though, microaggressions have been noted to adversely affect services delivered through helping relationships, such as therapy and counseling. When microaggressions occur during the process of counseling, counselors have been reported to be less skillful and have lower levels of multicultural competence; while the working alliance, critical to the counseling relationship, was reported to be weakened (Constantine, 2007).

Because microassualts, microinsults, and microinvalidations exist on a continuum, from overt and intentional to subtle and unintentional respectively, it seems that practitioners are at greatest risk for committing microinsults and microinvalidations when presenting parents with the feedback of psychoeducational evaluation results. For example, the practitioner might communicate surprise to parents when a student of limited financial resources scores high on a particular area of the evaluation (i.e. microinsult) or the practitioner attempts to calm a frustrated parent by stating "we just want what's best for the student" (i.e. microinvalidation). Although unintentional, these statements might be perceived by the parent to be judgmental and latently communicate lowered expectations of the student and the parent's desire for the student's success. Such communications will be detrimental to the working relationship with the parent-adversely affecting his or her ability to process the content of the feedback session and likely generating feelings of distrust towards the practitioner.

Implications for Practitioners: Developing Cultural Humility and Avoiding Microaggressions

The purpose of the feedback meeting is to share the results of the comprehensive psycho-educational evaluation with parents in a clear and understandable manner. The Feedback Model in-and-of-itself will accomplish this task; however, the practitioner will need to adjust the manner in which he or she presents when working with diverse families in order to be respectful of cultural differences and maintain a working rapport (Lamorey, 2002). To do so, the practitioner will need to have developed a sufficient degree of cultural humility in order to feel secure enough to openly admit limitations in his or her knowledge of the parents' racial and ethnic background and directly apologize if any microaggressions were intentionally or unintentionally committed during the feedback session. The ability to voluntarily accomplish these tasks in the moment during the feedback session will require the practitioner to first acknowledge personal deficits in his or her cultural humility and then actively pursue continuous professional development and supervision related to working with diverse families.

Researchers have suggested specific practices to facilitate the development of cultural humility in professional counselors (Hook et al., 2016). These practices, which emphasize practitioner introspection, continued education, and ongoing supervision, are directly applicable to all practitioners who wish to develop a greater sense of cultural humility and reduce the risk of committing microaggressions when working with diverse populations. Descriptions of each practice follow.

1) Practitioners should educate themselves on the broad concept of racial microaggressions, noting the various categories in which microaggressions can occur, and identifying the category in which they may be at greatest risk of committing a violation. The 12 categories of racial microaggressions that may occur in a therapeutic relationship are: a) colorblindness, b) overidentification, c) denial or personal racism, d) minimization of racial-cultural issues, e) assigning unique or special status on the basis of race or ethnicity, f) stereotyped assumptions about members of a racial or ethnic group, g) accused hypersensitivity regarding racial or cultural issues, h) meritocracy myth, i) culturally insensitive treatment considerations or recommendations, j) acceptance of suboptimal behaviors due to racial or cultural group membership, k) idealization, and l) patronizing (Constantine, 2007).

According to previous research, the most common racial microaggressions in the therapeutic relationship involved the denial of stereotypes or bias about cultural issues and the avoidance of discussion of cultural issues (Hook et al., 2016). Both of these microaggressions deny the reality of racial and ethnically diverse individuals; and they would damage the working rapport between practitioners and racial and ethnically diverse parents if they were to occur during a feedback session. As such, if racial or cultural concerns emerge from the parents during the feedback session, it would be best for the practitioner to directly engage the parent in dialogue, apologize, and directly admit his or her limitations in understanding nuances to the parents' cultural identity. Doing so would help support the goal of conducting a collaborative meeting and hopefully reduce the parents' anxiety to a degree that would allow them to adequately process the information to be communicated.

2) Practitioners should critically explore their personal stereotypes and biases about culture and race in an attempt to improve self-understanding and to deconstruct assumptions about various cultural group membership. Given our constant exposure to mainstream media and the fact that we are essentially "hard-wired" to be biased, the practitioner will need to devote intentional effort to continuously engage in this task, as he or she may need to challenge self-perceptions of privilege and meritocracy. Support from a mentor or trusted supervisor will be essential. The mentor or supervisor might encourage participation in structured multicultural educational opportunities and inspire routine relational engagement with culturally diverse individuals. More importantly though, the mentor or supervisor can gently confront the practitioner's beliefs about various cultures as they arise in daily practice.

3) Practitioners should generate and explore tactful strategies to address cultural issues that may arise during the feedback session in a humble and respectful manner that is sensitive to the parents' cultural identity. Although this task may seem daunting, it basically involves the willingness to engage in open dialogue with others who are perceived to be different. To do so, the practitioner will need to set aside his or her ideals, actively listen, and ask nonjudgmental questions as appropriate. If a misstep unintentionally occurs, then a sincere apology to the parents would be warranted and it would signify a willingness to learn and a continuous desire to deliver the feedback in a clear and understandable manner.

Summary

Working with racial, ethnic, and culturally diverse families will present a challenge for most practitioners. Those practitioners who do not recognize this challenge may "not know that they do not know;" whereas those who do recognize the challenge may continuously feel ill-equipped, unprepared, and ineffective. In the latter case, it is quite likely that these practitioners are holding themselves to the belief that they need to achieve some pre-determined minimal level of cultural competency or a discrete set of illusive skills that will unconditionally allow them to be effective practitioners with people of *all* races, ethnicities, and cultures. This is a flawed belief and it may ultimately promote stereotyping. It is virtually impossible for one to know *all* about the numerous races, ethnicities, and cultures that he or she may encounter in daily practice and listing the multitude of nuances and characteristics of various races, ethnicities, and cultures assumes that individuals in each group *all* have similar traits. As such, practitioners are encouraged to avoid setting unrealistic goals for themselves to achieve cultural competency and instead commit to the lifelong journey of pursuing cultural humility. Cultural humility has no endpoint, but instead is an ethos that involves introspection, self-critique, and engagement in on-going learning of those who are different from the practitioner. It assumes a position of non-superiority and hinges upon real-time dialogue with those of different racial, ethnic, and cultural backgrounds. It also protects against committing microaggressions or subtle comments or behaviors that will alienate parents of diverse backgrounds during the feedback process.

The current chapter began with a review of APA and NASP professional standards that defined ethically responsible service provision for diverse racial and ethnic groups. Afterwards, the concept of relational humility was introduced as a precursor to the discussion of cultural humility. The relationship between cultural humility and microaggressions was highlighted and microaggressions were defined and categorized into microassaults, microinsults, and microinvalidations. The adverse effects of microaggressions in counseling relationships were noted and recommendations to improve practitioners' cultural humility and to avoid committing microaggressions were offered. A goal of the current chapter was to present practitioners with an alternative view of working with parents of diverse racial, ethnic, and cultural background-strive to develop cultural humility as a versatile ethos that recognizes and respects the differences across the populations that we are charged to serve.

References

American Psychological Association (2017). *Ethical principles of psychologists and code of conduct* (2002, Amended June 1, 2010 and January 1, 2017). Retrieved from www.apa.org/ethics/code/index.aspx

Constantine, M. G. (2007). Racial microaggressions against African American clients in cross-racial counseling relationships. *Journal of Counseling Psychology, 54,* 1–16. http://dx.doi.org/10.1037/0022-0167.54.1.1

Davis, D. E., Hook, J. N., Worthington, E. L., Von Tongeren, D. R., Gartner, A. L., Jennings, D. J., & Emmons, R. A. (2011). Relational humility: Conceptualizing and measuring humility as a personality judgment. *Journal of Personality Assessment, 93*(3), 225–234.

Davis, D. E., Worthington, E. L., & Hook, J. N. (2010). Relational humility: A review of definitions and measurement strategies. *Journal of Positive Psychology, 5,* 243–252.

Davis, D. E., Worthington, E. L., Hook, J. N., Emmons, R. A., Hill, P. C., Bollinger, R. A., & Van Tongeren, D. R. (2013). Humility and the development and repair of social bonds: Two longitudinal studies. *Self and Identity, 12,* 58–77.

Gregg, A. P., Hart, C. M., Sedikides, C., & Kumashiro, M. (2008). Everyday conceptions of modesty: A prototype analysis. *Personality and Social Psychology Bulletin, 34,* 978–992.

Harrison, P. L. & Thomas, A. (2014). *Best practices in school psychology.* Bethesda, MD: National Association of School Psychologists.

Hook, J. N., Farrell, J. E., Davis, D. E., DeBlaere, C., Van Tongeren, D. R., & Utsey, S. O. (2016). Cultural humility and racial microaggressions in counseling. *Journal of Counseling Psychology, 63*(3), 269–277.

Kumagai, A. K. & Lypson, M. I. (2009). Beyond cultural competence: Critical consciousness, social justice, and multicultural education. *Academic Medicine, 84*(6), 782–787.

Lamorey, S. (2002). The effects of culture on special education services. Evil eyes, prayer meetings, and IEP's. *Teaching Exceptional Children, 34*(5), 67–71.

National Association of School Psychologists (2010). *Principles for professional ethics.* Bethesda, MD: Author. Retrieved from www.nasponline.org/standards/2010standards/1_%20Ethical%20Principles.pdf

National Association of School Psychologists (2013). *Racial and ethnic disproportionality in education.* Bethesda, MD: Author.

Sattler, J. M. (2014). *Foundations of behavior, social, and clinical assessment of children* (6th ed.). San Diego, CA: Jerome M. Sattler.

Sattler, J. M. (2018). *Assessment of children-cognitive foundations and application.* La Mesa, CA: Jerome M. Sattler.

Skiba, R. J., Poloni-Staudinger, L., Simmons, A., Feggins-Azzis, B., & Chung, C. G. (2005). Unproven links: Can poverty explain ethnic disproportionality in special education. *Journal of Special Education, 39*(3), 130–144.

Sue, D. W., Alsaidi, S., Awad, M. N., Glaeser, E., Calle, C. Z., & Mendez, N. (2019). Disarming racial microaggressions: Microintervention strategies for targets, white allies, and bystanders. *American Psychologist, 74,* 128–142. http://dx.doi.org/10.1037/amp0000296

Sue, D. W., Capodilupo, C. M., Torino, G. C., Bucceri, J. M., Holder, A. M. B., Nadal, K. L., & Esquilin, M. (2007). Racial microaggressions in everyday life: Implications for clinical practice. *American Psychologist, 62,* 271–286. http://dx.doi.org/10.1037/0003-066X.62.4.271

Tervalon, M. & Murray-Garcia, J. (1998). Cultural humility versus cultural competence: A critical distinction in defining physician training outcomes in multicultural education. *Journal of Health Care for the Poor and Underserved, 9*(2), 117–125.

Walcott, C. M., Charvet, J., McNamara, K. M., & Hyson, D. M. (2016). *School psychology at a glance: 2015 member survey results.* Bethesda, MD: National Association of School Psychologists. Retrieved from www.nasponline.org/.../Membership%20Survey%202015%20Handout.pdf

Yeager, K. A. & Bauer-Wu, S. (2013). Cultural humility: Essential foundation for clinical researchers. *Applied Nursing Research, 26*(4), 1–12. doi: 10.1016/j.apnr.2013.06.008

8 Application

The primary purpose of this text is to provide early career school psychologists and other practitioners who conduct psycho-educational evaluations with a concrete, parent-friendly Feedback Model that can be readily adapted to their school-based setting. This model is designed to help practitioners facilitate parents' understanding of evaluation results; thereby increasing parents' functional knowledge of their child's strengths and needs and reducing the risk of future parent-school conflict. While doing so, the text aims to describe critical elements to the process of providing feedback of psycho-educational evaluation results to parents, as related to relevant literature and practices in the areas of assessment, home-school relationships, and parents of children with disabilities.

The current chapter will present two case examples in which the Feedback Model is adapted to share the results of comprehensive psycho-educational evaluations. Both cases begin by sharing general background information and specific events preceding the feedback meeting. Afterwards, the feedback meetings are presented from the practitioner's perspective and commentary reviewing application of the Feedback Model is provided.

Case 1: Steven

Background Information

Steven is a 16-year-old ninth grade student who received a comprehensive psycho-educational evaluation as part of the triennial review of his Individual Education Plan. Steven has received special education services since 2013 when he was first identified to meet eligibility requirements for Specific Learning Disability, as defined by IDEA regulations.

Steven resides with his grandmother. He is the youngest of four children and his three older brothers reside outside of her home. English is the only language spoken in the home and information from the initial psycho-educational report noted a family history of learning disabilities, Attention Deficit Hyperactivity Disorder, and organic brain dysfunction.

At the time of initial evaluation (2013), Steven's overall level of intellectual functioning (Reynolds Intellectual Assessment Scales; RIAS) tested in the Average Range and commensurate with his Verbal and Nonverbal Intelligence Indices. His memory skills were measured in the Low Average Range and at a level consistent with performance on the Auditory Reasoning and Auditory Comprehension subtests of the Tests of Auditory Processing Skills-Third Edition (TAPS-III). As per the Wechsler Individual Achievement-Third Edition (WIAT-III) results, Steven's overall reading and written language skills were in the Low Average Range and significant difficulties were noted in the area of mathematics (Extremely Low Range). Although a slightly elevated depression subscale score was obtained on the teacher's version of the Behavior Assessment System for Children-Second Edition (BASC-II), significant social-emotional difficulties were not noted and overall adaptive functioning was rated to be in the Low Average Range (Global Adaptive Composite, Adaptive Behavior Assessment System-Second Edition, Teacher Form; ABAS-II).

Current Evaluation Results

According to the current evaluation results (2019), Steven's overall level of intellectual functioning tested in the upper limits of the Extremely Low Range (General Ability Index; Wechsler Intelligence Scale for Children-Fifth Edition; WISC-V) and commensurate with his Visual Spatial, Fluid Reasoning, Working Memory, and Processing Speed skills. Verbal comprehension skills were measured in the upper limits of the Very Low Range. Broad Reading and Written Language skills were measured in the Very Low and Extremely Low Ranges, respectively, and significant difficulties were noted in Mathematics (Extremely Low Range; Woodcock-Johnson Tests of Achievement-Fourth Edition; WJ-Ach-IV). Teacher ratings did not suggest significant social-emotional difficulties (BASC-III) and overall adaptive functioning scored within the Extremely Low Range (Global Adaptive Composite, Adaptive Behavior Assessment System-Third Edition; ABAS-III). Self-report data indicated interest in working with small animals after graduation. Patterns of performance on the current evaluation were consistent with previous results although lower; and data now suggested that Steven qualified for special education services as a student meeting the eligibility criteria for Intellectual Disability according to IDEA regulations.

Meeting Characteristics

The current evaluation results were planned to be shared at the time of Steven's triennial IEP meeting. This meeting occurred in the high school's conference room and was approximately 60 minutes in duration. The school psychologist, special education teacher (case manager), school counselor (serving as the administrative representative of the Local Education Agency), and physical education teacher were present. Steven's grandmother was unable to attend the IEP meeting because of a reported medical emergency and she provided consent for the meeting to proceed in her absence. The school psychologist was responsible for delivering the results of the psycho–educational evaluation to Steven and the team.

Student Meeting Prior to the Feedback Session

On the day of the feedback meeting, the practitioner met with the student beforehand for preparation purposes. The remaining sections of this case presentation are described from the practitioner's perspective.

Because I knew that this would be the first IEP meeting that Steven has attended, I briefly met with him that morning and talked him through the entire agenda. I explained the purpose of the meeting, who would be there, and what would be said. We also spoke of the general results of his assessment and I related them to the information that he had shared with me regarding his difficulties and successes in school. Because he qualified as a student with an Intellectual Disability, I also explained to him, in a honest and compassionate manner what that meant— "Learning is particularly challenging for you and it may take you longer to master skills than it may for other students." Upon checking for understanding, he shook his head in agreement and said, "Yes, this is me!" He went on to describe how difficult it is for him to learn new skills in math and reading. Initially, I was nervous to tell Steven that he had an Intellectual Disability, but I know now that this information helped him make sense of his daily struggles in school. Discussing his challenges and strengths informally prior to the meeting seemed to help Steven better understand the unique way in which he does learn, and the importance of his participation and presence in class activities (he often skipped class). Because I anticipated him asking if this meant that he was "stupid," we talked about his strengths and their connection to his future plans as an animal trainer. Doing so seemed to make the evaluation results more meaningful for him. During our conversation together, Steven seemed to comprehend the information being shared, as he verbalized connections between the results and his strengths and challenges.

Feedback Session with the IEP Team

Steven and I entered the meeting together (we were the first to arrive). I asked where he would prefer to sit and he chose to be at the head of the table. I sat to his right. Steven appeared to be relaxed and comfortable, and we spoke about how he was excited to be missing gym class "because running laps sucks." I agreed, and he laughed. The other meeting participants arrived shortly thereafter, and Steven's demeanor remained unchanged.

The case manager began the meeting. She explained the meeting's purpose and asked Steven if he had any questions about the agenda. Steven confidently replied, "I already know what all this is about … I don't have any questions." The case manager then signaled for me to begin and I turned and spoke directly to Steven. I reviewed the information his teachers had discussed with me. Steven occasionally interjected and agreed with what they had said regarding his frequent tardiness to class (from skipping and hanging out in the bathroom), his difficulty retaining concepts because of skipping class, as well as his confidence and willingness to support other students in class. I quietly asked Steven if he still felt up for sharing what he had spoken about with me about regarding his concerns about school and how he felt in class. Steven asked if I could tell them what he said. I turned to the others and shared how Steven reported to feel best supported when he is allowed to take short breaks. I also communicated Steven's interest in taking an art class, his worries about his grandmother's illness, and his future plans of becoming a dog trainer. I then turned to Steven and asked if there was anything else that he wanted me to share with the team and he smiled and shook his head indicating no.

I presented the information to Steven in consideration of his cognitive functioning. As such, the Feedback Model was altered to ensure better comprehension. In delivering the assessment results, my communication style with Steven was brief and concrete. I prioritized his voice and input to the team and frequently checked for Steven's understanding throughout the process.

On one side of a piece of paper I drew a giant brain and labeled it Steven's brain—he laughed. I then said, "When working together, we were looking to see how your brain works, what types of things you can remember, how fast you can copy those silly looking shapes, and the types of puzzles that you could complete." I then explained how Steven's performance on these tasks helped us understand his thinking skills and ability to adapt to his environment. I asked Steven if he knew the meaning of "adapt" and he shook his head "no." I explained that adapt meant how we adjust to the world around us, and he said, "Like how I sometimes put headphones on in class when people are being loud," and I said, "Exactly, that is a healthy strategy for adapting to a noisy environment."

I turned the paper over and said, "Let's talk about your thinking skills" and began to draw the graph while explaining the different ranges. To avoid confusion, I did not draw or explain categories above the Average Range, as Steven's highest score bordered the Low Average Range. "At the top of the paper is the Average Range—this is where you should be given your age. Then there is the Low Average Range—this is where you should be, but you require additional practice, more time, and may have difficulty with harder subjects. Next is the Very Low Range—this is where we start to say that your skills are underdeveloped. Do you know what underdeveloped means, Steven?" He said, "It means not good." I responded, "You're on the right track. It doesn't necessarily mean not good, it just means that your skills aren't fully developed, so scores that fall here will mean these areas are harder for you. Does that make sense?" He replied, "Yea." I continued stating, "and the Extremely Low Range—this is where we say that your skills are not where they should be given your age."

After the graph was drawn and the ranges were explained, I plotted and emphasized Steven's verbal comprehension index score. I explained that this score is the best predictor of how Steven may perform in the classroom, and it is just touching the Low Average Range. I reminded him of the VCI subtests and how he put forth effort and showed me his knowledge of words. I then proceeded to plot the VSI score in the Extremely Low Range. After doing so, I spoke about how this scale measured his "ability to think with shapes" and I asked him if he remembered making designs with blocks and finding the design that completed the puzzle in the book. Steven nodded yes when I mentioned the blocks. I then plotted his fluid reasoning score in the Extremely Low Range and said how this score "lets us know how well you can figure-out problems that you can't study for." Steven commented how he thought that he was better in this area and he pointed to the Average Range at the top of the graph. I reminded him of the "items with the scales" and the "puzzles with the hard shapes." Steven looked down at the table and I stated that these "were really hard for you." After several seconds of silence, I plotted the working memory and processing speed scores in the Extremely Low Range and stated to Steven how these scores "let us know how well you can pay attention and find special shapes while being timed." I then stated that "these scores suggest that your skills are below what would be expected, like you have difficulty with timed tasks and figuring out silly puzzles – this is like you were telling me about how you struggle in math and you feel like you often don't have enough time to complete your assignments in class." Steven went on to provide an anecdote about how just yesterday he became upset because his teacher (the present case manager) said to hand in an assignment he hadn't yet finished. The teacher then said to him that she was planning on handing the paper back that day for him to finish. Steven rolled his eyes. I turned to Steven and validated him mentioning these difficulties and again made clear the connection between what he'd said and the assessment results. "And remember how we spoke of that new word, adapt? Well, your ability to adapt to your environment is described by this graph. Sometimes it is hard for you, and you've shared that with us today, but I do want to highlight how particularly social, friendly, and helpful you are to the class, your friends, and other adults and students in this school. That is something you should be proud of, and those skills will be incredibly helpful to you in your future working with animals."

After plotting the WISC-V factor scores, I turned the paper over and drew a picture of a schoolhouse. Within the schoolhouse, I wrote "Reading," "Writing," and "Math." I then indicated how we were now going to look at how well he was able to do each. I turned the paper over and plotted the reading score while emphasizing how Steven did a nice job reading word lists and reading sentences aloud. I then plotted the Written Language score and explained how Steven was successful writing short sentences, especially when given word banks to use for each sentence. Afterwards, I plotted the Broad Mathematics score and shared how this score helps to explain the difficulties Steven has in math class. Steven shook his head in agreement while looking at the case manager.

With the graph of the cognitive and achievement results in front of Steven, I transitioned the conversation to explain the social-emotional and behavioral ratings. "And when we look at your behavior, others around you see you as pretty much a typical 16-year-old, in terms of your mood, ability to follow directions, and ability to make friends. However, we see that you have difficulty expressing yourself and figuring out basic tasks at home and at school."

After explaining the social-emotional and behavioral results, I reiterated to Steven that these results meant that he continues to be eligible for special education services and that he is eligible under the category of Intellectual Disability. He repeated to me that this means that it is harder for him to learn. I asked if he had any additional questions and he asked if he would continue to stay in the same class. His teacher interjected and responded "Yes." I asked Steven how that sounds to him, and he said that he likes to be in that class but spoke again about taking an art class. The counselor assured him that he would look into it.

Student and Team's Reaction to Feedback

As described, Steven participated in the feedback session and he appeared to be receptive and comfortable throughout the meeting. I am hopeful in his ability to self-advocate for himself in knowing his areas of success and difficulty. The team seemed pleasantly surprised with the delivery of the feedback results. While this particular method of delivery was unorthodox for this site, I felt that the meeting had a particular gentleness and lack of formality to it that made it seem more personal and accommodating for the student in which the meeting was about. The case manager later expressed interest in this model and suggested that I deliver results in this manner for all of my future feedback meetings.

Commentary

The purpose of sharing Steven's case was to illustrate the versatility of the Feedback Model. The evaluation results were originally planned to be shared with Steven's primary caregiver (grandmother); however, they were shared with the student because the grandmother was unable to attend the meeting. This practice is not necessarily unusual with high school students who have historically received special education services. Sharing the results with Steven posed unique challenges, as the practitioner needed to adapt the Feedback Model for it to be developmentally appropriate for Steven's understanding.

The practitioner is applauded for choosing to meet with Steven before the formal feedback meeting. This meeting helped to reestablish rapport with Steven and it provided him with a preview, or agenda, of the formal feedback meeting; thus helping to lower any anxiety and emotionally prepare for the content to be discussed and his interaction with other IEP team members in attendance. This meeting also provided the practitioner with a controlled opportunity to address any adverse reactions that Steven may have had towards his updated educational diagnosis of Intellectual Disability.

During both meetings with Steven, the practitioner intentionally used developmentally appropriate language to communicate the essence of the overall results. Rather than drawing-out the factor structure of the WISC-V and WJ-Achievement-Fourth Edition, the practitioner explained the instruments through drawings of a brain and schoolhouse, respectively. The practitioner also routinely checked for comprehension and Steven's responses to these inquiries suggested that he had a general understanding of higher-level concepts such as "adapt" and "underdeveloped." Of important note, the practitioner also chose to limit the number of categorical ranges explained on the graph, as Steven's performance bordered the lower limits of the Low Average Range. Doing so, helped to limit Steven's exposure to unnecessary details that could have potentially detracted from his understanding of the results.

It was clear that the feedback session was directed towards the student rather than the entire IEP team given the practitioner's verbalizations and behavior. Through doing so, the practitioner maintained a working rapport while communicating respect and value towards Steven; even though he was a student rather than an adult. Steven's comments throughout the meeting suggested that he had a basic understanding of the evaluation results at the conclusion of the feedback session and other team members seemed impressed with the manner in which the evaluation results were presented to the student and the team.

Case 2: Teresa

Background Information

Teresa is a 14-year 2-month-old 8th grade student who received a comprehensive psycho-educational evaluation as part of a triennial review of her Individual Education Plan. Teresa has received special education services since 2013 when she was first identified to meet eligibility requirements for Intellectual Disability and Speech Language Impairment, as defined by IDEA regulations.

Teresa resides with her biological parents and older sister and brother. Teresa is of Latino and Native American origin. Spanish is the only language spoken in the home and Teresa reportedly "thinks" and regularly watches television in Spanish. Information from the initial psycho-educational report noted an uncomplicated pregnancy and delays in meeting developmental milestones. Teresa's brother was also noted to have a history of learning disabilities.

At the time of initial evaluation (2013), the Kaufman Assessment Battery for Children-Second Edition (KABC-II) yielded Nonverbal and Mental Processing Indices the Lower Extreme Range, commensurate scores in the areas of Sequential Processing, Simultaneous Processing, and Planning, and Average performance in the Learning domain. Academic skills in Broad Reading, Broad Mathematics, and Broad Written Language were consistent and within the Very Low Range (Woodcock-Johnson Tests of Achievement-Third Edition; WJ-Ach-III) and overall adaptive functioning was rated within the Extremely Low Range (Adaptive Behavior Assessment System-Second Edition, Teacher Form; ABAS-II). Furthermore, the speech and language evaluation conducted by the Speech and Language Pathologist indicated that Teresa showed delay in understanding and using language in both Spanish and English as her scores fell below the 7th percentile rank.

Current Evaluation Results

According to the current evaluation results (2019), Teresa's Nonverbal Index of the Kaufman Assessment Battery for Children-Second Edition (KABC-II) scored in the Lower Extreme Range and Broad Reading, Broad Mathematics, and Broad Written Language skills were measured in the Very Low Range (Woodcock-Johnson Tests of Achievement-Fourth Edition; WJ-Ach-IV). Adaptive behavior functioning continued to be within the Extremely Low Range (Adaptive Behavior Assessment System-Third Edition, Teacher Form; ABAS-III) and results from the speech language pathologist again noted delay in understanding and using language in both Spanish and English.

Meeting Characteristics

The current evaluation results were planned to be shared at the time of Teresa's triennial IEP meeting. This meeting occurred in the middle school's conference room and was approximately 60 minutes in duration. In addition to Teresa's father, the school psychologist, special education teacher (case manager), school counselor (serving as the administrative representative of the Local Education Agency), general education math teacher, speech-language pathologist, and social-worker who served as a translator were present. The speech language pathologist was responsible for delivering the results of the speech-language evaluation and the school psychologist was charged with delivering the results of the psycho-educational evaluation to Teresa's father and the team.

Initial Interactions Prior to the Feedback Session

The remaining sections describing this case are presented from the practitioner's perspective.

Prior to the feedback session, I practiced the Feedback Model in its entirety with the social worker. Together, we each had a copy of the psycho-educational report and we both made notes of the important parts to highlight in each of the sections. Her support better prepared me in how to present this information to the parent in a way that not only made sense to him, but didn't overwhelm. Overall, this served to promote a much smoother presentation delivery of the results during the actual feedback meeting.

On the day of the feedback meeting, the social worker and I waited outside of the conference room for the father to arrive. When he arrived, the social worker guided introductions before we moved into the meeting room where the other professionals were already seated. The father sat at the head of the table, with the social worker to his right and I to his left. The father seemed somewhat uncomfortable, as he appeared jittery. The father never stopped smiling throughout the entire meeting and I attributed this behavior to nervousness or uneasiness that he may have felt while being in the presence of the team members seated around the table.

Feedback Session with the IEP Team

The case manager began the meeting. He explained the meeting's purpose and asked Teresa's father if he had any questions about the agenda. After this content was translated, the father shook his head no. The speech language pathologist interjected and asked if he could present the speech language results first because he needed to leave. The speech language pathologist looked and spoke to everyone except for Teresa's father. He spoke quickly about wanting to exit Teresa from services given her chronological age and limitations to her development. The content was translated and the father nodded his head and said "thank you." The case manager then motioned to me to begin sharing the results. Speaking directly to Teresa's father, I shared that we would be reviewing evaluation results that help describe Teresa's performance in the classroom setting. After translation, he responded, "Yes, that's fine." I then pointed out how Teresa was polite and she persevered with evaluation tasks throughout our sessions, noting that these behaviors are sometimes less pronounced with other 14-year-olds. I also thanked him again for attending the meeting given his busy work schedule. After translation, the father nodded his head, smiled, and said "thank you."

Throughout the remainder of the feedback session, I continued to speak directly to Teresa's father, stating one to two sentences and allowing opportunity for translation. My goal was to present the results to the father in a manner that was sensitive to his level of understanding and malleable for easy translation. As such, verbiage of the Feedback Model was modified and I used basic Spanish terms during my explanation whenever possible. I began by reviewing the information shared by Teresa's teachers. Teacher comments were overwhelmingly positive, namely that Teresa is a hard worker and a leader in class. After the information was translated, Teresa's father shook his head in agreement, smiled, and said "thank you." I then proceeded to explain how all of the results that we are going to describe today were obtained by comparing Teresa's performance to other 14-year-two-month-old students.

On one side of a blank piece of paper, I drew a giant brain and labeled it Teresa's "cerebro." Inside the brain image, I wrote "rompecabezas" (puzzles), "numeros" (numbers), and "memoria" (memory) and said "While working together, Teresa was asked to complete visual and number puzzles as well as complete memory and other timed tasks." Upon translation, Teresa's father smiled and made eye contact.

I turned the paper over and drew the graph while explaining the different ranges. I only drew the Average to Very Low Ranges given the distribution of Teresa's overall pattern of performance. These were labeled as follows: Promedio, Debajo de Promedio, Bajo, and Muy Bajo.

At the top of the paper is the Promedio Range—this is where a student should be given her age. Then there is the Debajo de Promedio Range—this is also where a student should be, but they may require additional practice, more time, may have difficulty with more challenging subjects … Bajo—this is where we say that a student's skills are underdeveloped. And Muy Bajo—this is where we say that a student's skills are below where they should be given their age.

The translator offered additional comment and Teresa's father smiled. I then plotted Teresa's Nonverbal Index score in the Muy Bajo Range and briefly described the related subtests of this composite.

Teresa's performance on these tasks indicate that her abilities to solve visual and number puzzles, use short term memory, and complete timed tasks are below where we would expect given her age which means that she learns slower than other students.

Upon translation, Teresa's father looked at the graph and I asked if there were any questions. The translator shook her head no. I then turned the paper with the graph and wrote in three columns "lectura amplia" (broad reading), "matematicas generales" (broad mathematics), and "legua escrita amplia" (broad written language). While pointing to lectura amplia, I stated,

> While working with Teresa, we asked her to read word lists of increasing difficulty, supply the missing word to a sentence or paragraph in order for it to make sense, respond true or false to simple sentences within a time limit, and read lists of nonsense words of increasing difficulty.

After translation was provided, I turned the paper over and plotted "lectura amplia" in the Muy Bajo Range on the graph. I turned the paper over and while pointing to "matematicas generales," I stated the following.

> In the broad area of mathematics, Teresa was asked to complete math word problems using paper and pencil, solve math problems of increasing difficulty, and respond to basic arithmetic problems within a time limit.

Translation was then provided and I turned the paper over plotted "matematicas generales" in the Muy Baho Range on the graph. Teresa's father stared at the graph and indicated that he did not have any questions after being prompted by the translator. I turned the paper over and while pointing to legua escrita amplia stated,

> In the broad area of written language, Teresa was required to spell words of increasing difficulty dictated by the examiner, compose appropriate sentences after provided prompts, and write as many sentences as possible within a time limit when provided word banks.

After translation was provided, I turned the paper over and plotted "lengua escrita amplia" in the Muy Baho Range on the graph. While pointing across the plots of her cognitive and academic functioning on the graph, I emphasized that Teresa's cognitive functioning and academic skills are similar and significantly underdeveloped when compared to others of similar age. Teresa's father smiled at me after translation and I proceeded to discuss the adaptive behavior scores.

> Because of where her cognitive and academic skills fall on the graph, we needed to examine Teresa's adaptive behavior functioning. Teresa's adaptive behavior was measured through teacher ratings and these ratings tell us how well Teresa gets-along in her environment when compared to others of similar age.

Translation was provided and I then plotted "comportamiento adaptativo" (adaptive behavior) in the Muy Baho Range. Teresa's father pointed across the scores on the graph, looked at me, and shook his head yes. While referring to the graph, I pointed-out how these scores are similar to the results that were obtained in the past and stated that Teresa continues to qualify for special education services under the category of Intellectual Disability. I paused and asked the father if he had any questions. After translation, the father stated no.

Parent and Team's Reaction to Feedback

At the conclusion of the feedback meeting, Teresa's father expressed his gratefulness for work done with Teresa and he seemed pleased with Teresa's teachers and the progress that she has made in school. He did not ask any questions throughout the process. I am unsure if this was because he genuinely did not have any questions, if he did not understand, or if he was uncomfortable asking. The case manager and I met briefly after the meeting. At this time, the case manager described how he was pleasantly surprised with the feedback method and he appreciated how I spoke directly to the parent and at a pace that allowed for translation. The case manager was particularly happy with the visual representation of scores, as he felt that this method is much easier for parents to understand in comparison to simply reading the psycho-educational report or using a bell-curve visualization to describe the student's performance.

Commentary

The purpose of sharing Teresa's case was to demonstrate how the Feedback Model can be utilized with parents who speak a language other than English. With the support of a translator, utilization of basic visual-aids, and translation of the categorical ranges and constructs measured, it appears that the practitioner adequately communicated the evaluation results to the parent in a manner that was reasonably understandable. The practitioner held a meeting with the translator before the formal feedback session in order to familiarize the translator with the results and to prepare the translator for the general flow of the feedback session. This meeting was believed to be of great value because it created a working rapport between both professionals and helped the translator better understand the communication style of the practitioner. More importantly though, the meeting likely helped reduce any anxiety that the practitioner and translator may have had prior to the feedback session; thereby reducing the potential for the transference of anxiety onto the parent during the time of the formal meeting.

The practitioner and translator are commended for greeting the father outside of the meeting room and accompanying him into the feedback session. This action likely helped to reduce the father's anxiety and help him feel more comfortable entering a room where others are already seated around the table. Throughout the feedback session, the practitioner spoke directly to the parent and avoided the default of only communicating with the translator. This practice conveyed respect to the father and hopefully helped him to feel more comfortable and included in the meeting. The practitioner plotted the broad composite scores and explained the various tasks (subtests) that comprised each score. This manner of describing Teresa's performance was succinct and it avoided unnecessary details that could have overloaded the father's short-term working memory especially since translation was required. If Teresa's performance on the individual subtests that comprised each composite score was noteworthy in terms of identifying particular strengths or difficulties, then it would have been appropriate for the practitioner to plot the subtest scores in the same columns of the related composite scores on the graph.

Because the parent did not speak English or share a common culture with others at the feedback meeting, the practitioner likely experienced difficulty determining whether or not he truly understood the results that were communicated. In such cases, the practitioner is at risk of too frequently asking, "Do you understand?" or "Do you have any questions?" Asking these questions too frequently could precipitate anxiety on behalf of the parent, as the parent may be thinking "I don't have any questions, but should I" or "If I don't have any questions, does that tell them that I don't care about my child?" With these circumstances, the practitioner needs to trust the parent as an adult and assume that he or she would ask questions if truly necessary.

Summary

The current chapter presented two cases examples in which the Feedback Model was adapted to share the results of comprehensive psycho-educational evaluations. Both cases began by sharing general background information and specific events preceding the feedback meeting. Afterwards, each feedback meeting was described from the practitioner's perspective and commentary reviewing application of the Feedback Model followed.

Each case presented with its own unique challenges. With Steven's case, the practitioner was required to deliver the feedback of evaluation results to a 16-year-old student who met eligibility criteria for Intellectual Disability, as his grandmother was unable to attend the meeting. The practitioner adapted the Feedback Model to make it suitable for the student's understanding through limiting complex details and utilizing more concrete visual aids to describe the cognitive and achievement measures. Verbalizations and nonverbal behaviors throughout the feedback process suggested that Steven had a basic understanding of the evaluation results at the conclusion of the meeting. Alternatively, with Teresa's case, the practitioner needed to work collaboratively with a translator to deliver the feedback of evaluation results to a Spanish speaking parent. In this example, the practitioner relied on concrete visuals, minimized unnecessary details, and translated the descriptive ranges of the graph into Spanish to help facilitate parent understanding. Verbalizations and nonverbal behaviors of the parent during the feedback process suggested a basic understanding of the evaluation results; however, one might suspect that the parent may have asked questions or participated more regularly during the meeting if communication barriers did not exist.

9 Conclusion

The purpose of this text was to provide early career school psychologists and other practitioners who conduct psycho-educational evaluations with a concrete, parent-friendly Feedback Model that can be readily adapted to their school-based setting. This model was designed to facilitate parents' understanding of evaluation results; thereby increasing their functional knowledge of their child's strengths and needs and reducing the risk of future parent-school conflict. While doing so, the text described critical elements to the process of providing feedback of psycho-educational evaluation results to parents, as related to relevant literature and practices in the areas of assessment, home-school relationships, and parents of children with disabilities.

The text began by presenting an underlying rationale of the Feedback Model and reasons that support its daily use were discussed. Afterwards, the Information Processing Model of human learning was reviewed while relating its principles to the Feedback Model's infrastructure. With this knowledge, parents' stressors and perceptions of the feedback meeting were discussed and prerequisite practitioner skills to utilizing the Feedback Model was reviewed. The Feedback Model was then presented in a detailed stepwise manner and specific verbiage for each step was provided. Utilizing the model with diverse populations was subsequently reviewed and the text concluded with two case examples in which the Feedback Model was applied.

School psychologists and other mental health professionals who conduct comprehensive psycho-educational evaluations are ethically obligated to share the evaluation results in a clear and understandable manner with parents and clients. Despite this fact, many practitioners receive limited training to develop this skill in comparison to the training received regarding assessment administration, scoring, interpretation, and report writing. Presenting psycho-educational evaluation results is akin to delivering an instructional lesson. Preparation, awareness of audience needs, and organization are essential. In addition to possessing cultural self-awareness and humility, practitioners need to have knowledge of human learning principles, sensitivity towards the needs of parents and families of children with disabilities, and fluency in describing standardized assessment instruments and the related constructs measured. The Feedback Model integrates each of these concepts and provides practitioners with a much needed tool that can grow with their future practice and experience.

Index

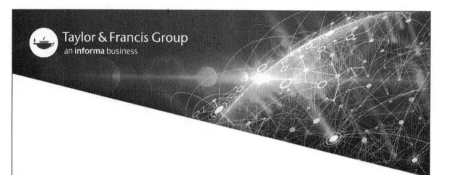